Author's Note: The views and opinions expressed in this book are those of the author only and do not reflect those of any specific NGO or organisation. For legal reasons, the organisation I worked for has been changed, and extensive edits have been made to protect privacy and confidentiality. True names, descriptions, and the genuine recovery process have been altered. It is important to note that being authentic and sharing the truth was of utmost importance to me. However, due to a breach in the code of conduct, I have had to make necessary changes in accordance with the guidelines provided. I deeply regret that I am unable to provide the full truth and share the name of the organisation that I hold in high regard as the best career experience I've had to date. This book was initially intended for my own mental recovery and health, but it has evolved into a narrative that I believe can offer inspiration and help others. I hope that my experiences motivate you to live a life worth remembering.

This book includes references to several sensitive subjects, including violence and suicidal thoughts, which some readers may find upsetting or otherwise triggering. Every effort has been made to approach these subjects with sensitivity and respect. If you or someone you know is experiencing a mental health crisis or suicidal behaviour, seek help immediately by calling the National Suicide and Crisis Lifeline (dial 13 11 14 in Australia or 988 in the United States).

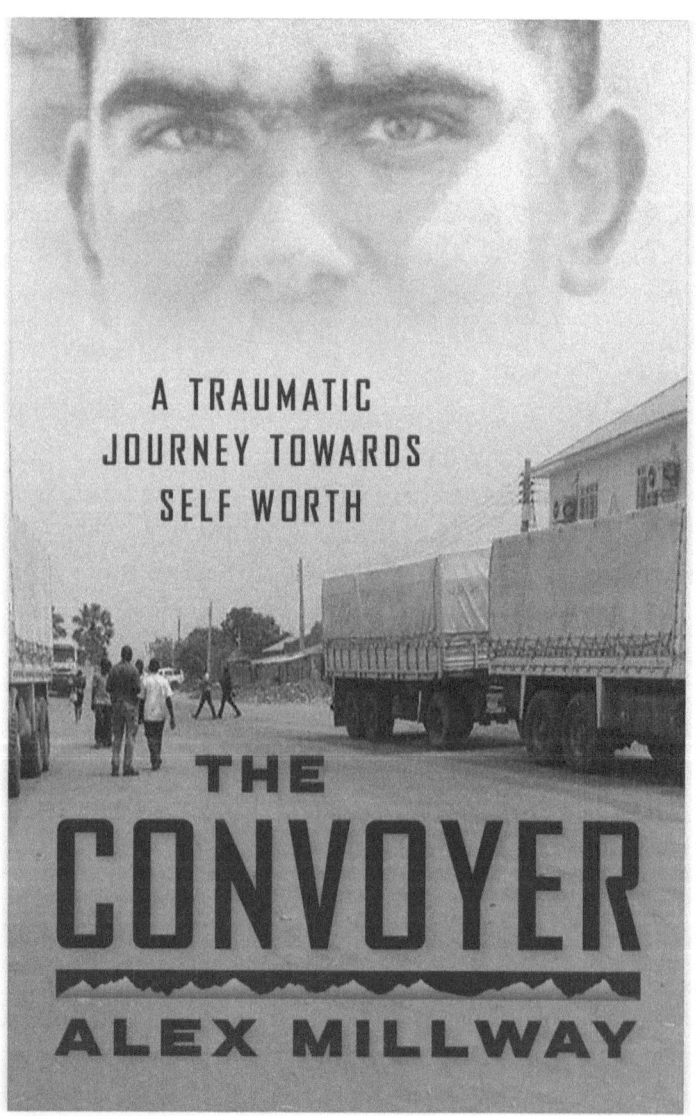

original cover version 1.0

AM I WORTHY

AM I WORTHY

ALEX MILLWAY

COPYRIGHT © 2024 ALEX MILLWAY
All rights reserved.

AM I WORTHY
A Traumatic Journey toward Self-Worth

FIRST EDITION

ISBN   978-1-5445-3572-2   *Hardcover*
        978-1-5445-3570-8   *Paperback*
        978-1-5445-3571-5   *Ebook*

FOR ALL THOSE WHO DIED, BEFORE, DURING, AND AFTER.
YOU HAVE EACH SHAPED MY LIFE IN ONE WAY OR ANOTHER.

IN NO PARTICULAR ORDER

Michael
Mick
Shorts
Nicolas
Salah Dudu
Alexi
Alex
Macca
Shadrak

CONTENTS

FOREWORD..11

CHAPTER 1..17

CHAPTER 2.. 33

CHAPTER 3..51

CHAPTER 4..75

CHAPTER 5..97

CHAPTER 6..123

CHAPTER 7..133

CHAPTER 8 151

CHAPTER 9..165

FOREWORD

—TOBI GRIFFITHS

I FIRST MET ALEX MILLWAY IN 2012. WE'D BOTH ENLISTED in the Australian Defense Force and were assigned to the same platoon. From the start, it was clear he was more mature than most of the new recruits. After basic training, we were both transferred to the same facility for Initial Employment Training, or IET. That's where our friendship really began. We bonded through our experiences as new soldiers and our previous travel adventures. I saw then the ways Alex can be a *grey man*: present but unnoticed in a group of people. He tends to sit back and observe social situations rather than jumping right in. He's open, warm, and friendly; he's also very calculated and shrewd. It doesn't take him long to get a read on people or to analyse a situation. He's also very goal oriented. When some soldiers learn they're going to be deployed to the Middle East, they experience anxiety. Not Alex. When he received news of his deployment, he was excited and saw in it the opportunity for achievement and the chance to be of service.

Those attributes are really at the core of who he is. No matter the situation, Alex Millway is humble, generous, and compassionate. It doesn't matter if you are a lifelong friend or he just met you two minutes ago: he'll treat you with the same warmth and consideration. Amongst our group of mates, we joke that Alex makes the rest of us look bad, since he never forgets a birthday or fails to show up with a gift. He's also the source of incredible inspiration. I look up to Millway like an older brother, and he's always been there for me, no matter the situation. I love knowing that he'll give me the honest truth, even if I don't want to hear it. He motivates me to be a better person, whether that's embracing travel or volunteering in my community. And he celebrates every little achievement of mine, whether it's hitting a fitness goal or donating blood. "You're doing amazing," he'll say, as if I've just qualified for the Olympics or won the Nobel Peace Prize.

Alex's entire professional life has been dedicated to helping and supporting people, whether he's met them before or not. Sometimes that commitment to others has put him at real risk. Alex is the kind of person who focuses on the end goal more than the potential danger required to get there. He'll walk through just about any kind of risk in the name of helping someone. As a result, he's experienced a level of trauma that would break most average people. Millway, on the other hand, tends to take that kind of stress on the chin and gets right back to doing what he loves the most. If he has a flaw, it's that he sometimes forgets to look out for himself in the process.

It took a while before I understood where Alex Millway gets some of his motivation. As you'll read in this book, his childhood was far from easy. Even as a young boy, he experienced a level of trauma few people have had to endure. Millway learned early on that the only real advocate or support system he had was himself. With that kind of upbringing, you learn quickly that failure is not an option: there is no emotional (or even financial) safety net, even if you need one. It wasn't until I read *The Convoyer* that I realised just how much this kind of trauma has impacted Alex and other people with similar backgrounds. I don't know that I could have gone through everything he's experienced and come out the other side with the same amount of compassion, strength, and humour as Alex has.

I will never forget the night Millway called me after he'd been ambushed while working for the ▮▮▮▮▮▮▮ in South Sudan. I was out in Melbourne with some friends, clubbing and having some drinks, when I saw an unknown number appear on my phone. Normally, I'd ignore that kind of call, but something told me I should answer this one. The minute I heard Alex's voice, I knew it was serious. It was pretty daunting to hear the one man I really look up to say that he was afraid. Hearing the fear in his voice as he described being held at gunpoint by rebels and wondering if he and his team were going to be executed was sobering to say the least. True to his nature, Alex's first concern was making sure that his siblings and other loved ones didn't learn about the ambush on the news. He asked me to notify them—and to make sure they knew that he was safe.

The next few days were stressful. I didn't hear from Millway, and I had no way of contacting him or knowing if he was okay. When we finally spoke, Alex tried shaking off the incident like it was no big deal. He told me they were planning on sending him out on another mission, and I didn't bother trying to hide my concern. But Alex downplayed the danger: "We've got a job to do," he told me. It would be much later before he realised just how impacted he'd been by the ambush and the degree to which post-traumatic stress disorder (PTSD) had taken over his operating systems. That's the thing about PTSD: it rarely looks like Hollywood depictions of the condition. Instead, in Alex's case, it seemed more like a gradual backing off as he slipped further and further into his shell.

Much of *The Convoyer* is Millway's first-person account of this trauma and how he overcame it. When he first told me he was writing a book, I was thrilled. This story will benefit so many people, whether or not they've experienced PTSD themselves. It's a narrative about the importance of living your life and your passions and how to come back from the brink. It's about fighting for what you believe in and the importance of getting help when it's needed. Millway's story is a powerful reminder that no one who has experienced trauma of any sort is alone. The bravery he demonstrates in these pages will help all kinds of people. That's important. Too many people—especially men—are taught to bury their feelings or to just suck it up when things get hard. We're socialised to think that getting help is a sign of weakness rather than strength. Back when Millway and I joined the military, we were trained to do the same.

The Convoyer has important lessons for other people as well. The thing I love the most about this book is that every reader will interpret the events of Alex Millway's life differently. While I related to his stories about the military, others might identify more with his travel narratives, stories about his family, or his path towards personal acceptance. It doesn't matter what kind of lifestyle you've been given or what your background is like. It also doesn't matter what makes you happy, or what gives you a sense of purpose and passion: *The Convoyer* has a message for you as well. Watching Alex experience life in developing nations and seeing his experience in war-torn regions is an important wake-up call for all of us. It's a lesson in how we should all embrace life and do what we love.

This book is also a reminder about the importance of never judging a book by its cover. One of the most important messages I got from reading *The Convoyer* is how you can know someone for many years without ever realising how much they've gone through or what kind of trauma they've experienced. Reading Alex Millway's story was a real wake-up call for me. I realise now just how important it is to check in on my friends and to take the time needed to truly understand their life and their experiences. Reading what Alex actually went through has definitely encouraged me to build stronger relationships with the people I care about. It's taught me that everybody needs help eventually. Not only do I feel more committed than ever to becoming that support for my loved ones, but I've also realised how important it is for me to ask for help from them as well.

The Convoyer will definitely make you think. If you're like me, you'll probably find yourself reading a few pages and then wanting to put it down and reflect on the wisdom Millway offers. It's not a particularly massive book in terms of pages, but the insight here is huge. I'm also certain that it's not the end of Alex's story. He has a lifetime of adventure ahead of him, and I can't wait to read where it takes him next. After reading *The Convoyer*, I think you'll feel the same.

CHAPTER 1

@THECONVOYER

QR code for Instagram videos and colourised graphics.

I SPENT MY EARLY YEARS IN VÉSENAZ, SWITZERLAND, A charming old Alpine village not far from Lake Geneva. I don't have a particularly detailed or vivid recollection of my early childhood there: much of it is blurry, or perhaps suppressed. However, there are a few pleasant memories from that time, which remind me that parts of my childhood were happy and carefree.

House in Vésenaz.

Everything in Vésenaz was within walking distance, so even as a young boy I could quite easily get myself to school, to the shops, and to my friends' houses. One of my best friends at the time, Clara, lived particularly close, just on the other side of a vineyard. During the grape harvest, the vineyard owners would put nets out to protect the grapes, and from time to time, birds would get stuck in there. Whenever we would see the birds stuck, we would sneak over and cut holes in the nets to set the birds free. Beyond Clara's house there was a stable, where she took lessons. I began taking lessons there as well, and after riding classes we'd walk to a nearby bakery where we'd use our pocket change to purchase a *pain au lait*, or chocolate croissant.

Our school was in a grassy area filled with big millipedes (they turned out to be dangerous, but we didn't know it at the time). Throughout the village itself, the streets were lined with trees everywhere, and the whole area was very lush. Most of the houses in our village were made out of brick, and many looked the same to me. Their yards were filled with huge hedges—two metres high on each side—and big, formal gardens. Our home was also very expansive: a five-storey mansion that was split into two residences. We occupied the back end of the house, and neighbours had the front end. Despite sharing the home, we had a ton of space to ourselves, and my siblings and I loved playing in the yard, which was huge. Set on a hill, it was a perfect place to toboggan in the wintertime. During the summer, I'd search for hedgehogs amongst the tall trees or work on building a new tree house.

Family photograph of me, Sonia, Lea, Mother, and Jeffrey on a hike in the Swiss Alps.

I shared the house with my mother, stepfather, and three siblings. My brother, Jeffrey, is the eldest, and then there's our sister, Lea. My twin sister, Sonia, and I are the youngest. You might not guess that Sonia and I are twins since we look quite different. While I have dark brown hair and darker skin, she is blonde and fair. We certainly have the twin bond though. Growing up, I was the cheeky one: I was always the one chatting up strangers or using strange voices to get people's attention. I loved telling jokes or inventing my own languages, anything to get a reaction from people.

We were all in vitro fertilisation (IVF) babies, so you might assume that my mother wanted us all badly, but that never felt like the case. Amongst the four of us, there were seemingly no favourites—no one who dodged our mother's erratic behaviour and withering criticism. Perhaps she was just doing the best she knew how, but most of the time it felt like she wished she'd never had us. I could never understand how she could go through the IVF process repeatedly, then not want any of us once we were born.

Often, I felt like our mother wanted me the least. Our mother always said that she and our father initially only wanted two kids, but then they thought, *Okay, we'll have one more.* Unexpectedly, they became pregnant with twins. I was born second, which made me the extra one. I worried constantly that I was unwanted. When I would ask if I was a mistake, my mother would always matter-of-factly say, "Yes." I don't remember her ever trying to reassure me otherwise.

I never had much of a relationship with my real father. My parents divorced very early in my life, and I don't have any memories of him in Switzerland. My siblings tell me that initially we continued to meet up with him for visitations in public parks before he left for a new life in Australia. However, I don't remember any of them. Instead, there's a gap in my mind where memories of loving time spent with my father ought to be. That sense of not being wanted by either of my parents would set the course for my life in unimaginable ways. It would lead me to seek adventure around the world and ultimately to place my life in danger, all in a quest to find self-worth and a sense of belonging. Even as a young child, I was plagued by the fear that I didn't really matter. If you experienced any kind of trauma as a child, you may understand what I mean. That lack of attachment and acceptance as a young child can easily set the stage for a lifetime of questioning one's self-worth.

Me making a gingerbread house.

To make matters worse, the house we lived in was actually owned by our stepfather, Louis. My mum married Louis when

Sonia and I were about two years old. There was a twenty-one-year age gap between him and my mum, and he always seemed so much older. She was tanned and fit, with brown eyes and hair, which she kept cut in a youthful bob that grazed her neckline. She wore bohemian clothes and silver jewellery, which also made her seem younger than she actually was. Louis, on the other hand, was pale and overweight, with grey hair and a bald spot. When I think back on him, I remember a man who was, at best, distant. He rarely took opportunities to have a father–son moment or to interact with the three of us. The only thing I ever remember him really teaching me was how to shave when I was about seven. Even that interaction was brief and not very engaging. Louis was never really present for us as a family—as a stepfather, as a guardian, as a friend, or anything else. Looking back, it's as if Louis were a stranger or just someone who happened to live with us.

Despite the massive amount of space we had at home, the house soon began to feel crowded with the conflict and anger brewing between my mum and stepdad. It spilled over onto us kids in all kinds of ways. I remember one particularly bad Christmas when I was about four years old. That morning, the family gathered in the living room to open presents. It was snowing, and my siblings and I were excited because, after presents, we'd get to go outside in our backyard and play in the snow. In the meantime, we were all enjoying the Christmas tree—the last one I remember having in any home until I moved out on my own at the age of eighteen. Under the tree was a special present for me: a little helicopter toy that had a plastic stand and a remote control for speed and direction. It was quite simple, but I loved that little helicopter and immediately began playing with it. However, it didn't take long until my stepdad announced he'd had enough.

"That thing is too noisy," he said. "You've got to get rid of it."

"You can't take it away," I protested. "It's not fair."

I continued playing with the new helicopter, but he got angry at me again. So, I put down the toy and went outside to play in the snow. I stayed in the yard for a bit, climbing trees, but I hadn't bundled up, so it wasn't long before I heard my mother's voice: "You're going to catch a cold! Come back inside!"

When I came back inside, the helicopter was gone.

"What happened to my toy?" I asked.

"It's broken," my stepfather told me. "It doesn't work anymore."

He showed me the helicopter, and he was right: nothing was working on it. I went to my room and started playing with Legos or some other toys I'd gotten that day. The next morning, it occurred to me that the helicopter was battery-powered. I located the remote control for the TV in the living room, removed its batteries, and put them into my toy. What do you know, but it started working again. I was so overjoyed to be reunited with my gift that it never occurred to me that taking the batteries out of a stepfather's remote control was not a good thing to do. The fierceness of his reaction surprised me.

"How did you get this to work?" he shouted as soon as I started circling the helicopter around again.

"I took the batteries from the remote control," I explained.

Before I understood what was happening, I was being yelled at and sent to my room. The next time I came downstairs, I couldn't find the toy anywhere. I was given no explanation other than that it was gone. Even then, I knew Louis had gotten rid of it just because it bothered him. That was a defining moment in my childhood. From then on, I realised that if people didn't like something of mine, they would take it away, no matter how much I liked it. I started playing with anything I enjoyed somewhere private, like my room, because I couldn't trust that anyone else would allow me to have it.

Louis's wrath wasn't just reserved for me. And not only did it extend to my siblings, but sometimes my friends experienced it as well. Every year in mid-December, the communities around Geneva celebrate *L'Escalade*, a festival commemorating a seventeenth-century battle. Our school would mark the occasion with a big chocolate *marmite* (or cauldron); each year, the youngest and oldest child would hit the cauldron with a hammer, and out would pour all kinds of treats. Every child from the school would get a piece of chocolate, some maison biscuits, and a lolly. We'd also have soup as part of the tradition and would dress up in silly clothing for the holiday as well. One year, Clara and her sister stopped by before school so that we could walk to the celebration together. To this day, we have no idea what set off Louis, but he began yelling at Clara, berating her for some imagined offence. She started to cry, and even that didn't soften his anger. Before that moment, I hadn't realised Louis yelled at anyone besides me and my siblings. I felt terrible for Clara; we were only little kids, and there's no way she had done anything to deserve that treatment.

Louis's rage was also directed at my mother. She had her own terrible temper, and it didn't take long before the tension between them became unmanageable. Often, it would erupt in epic arguments. On one particularly bad instance, we'd all gone for a hike up in the mountains. Sonia and I were only about six years old, but we took the lead, excited to be in the alpine forest. The rest of the family lagged behind on the unpaved, rocky trail. We hadn't made it far when we heard Louis shout out in pain. Turns out he'd stumbled and hurt his ankle quite badly.

As we returned to the car, my mum and Louis began arguing about something. I'm sure his mood was made worse by his ankle, and he gradually fell well behind the rest of the family. Once we reached the car, my mum and the four of us kids piled inside. Without waiting for my stepfather, she turned on the ignition and began pulling away without him. We made it up the road to a roundabout, while he continued stumbling behind us, trying to keep up on foot. When we slowed down at the roundabout, Louis somehow managed to catch up. He whacked the car with his hand—so aggressively that it scared all us kids. My mum still somehow managed to ignore him and continued driving ahead, oblivious to both the other drivers and the angry husband shouting behind her. We were getting honked at as we cut people off, but all I could think about was how mad Louis had gotten and how seemingly strange my mother was acting. The fear I experienced because of her behaviour stuck with me for a long time.

Today, my siblings and I still believe that my stepfather's stumble in the forest was the beginning of the end of their marriage, though it may have been deteriorating well before that and without our knowledge. The fact is that my siblings and I were too young at the time to really understand what was happening. And at that age, we didn't know enough about adult relationships to realise how dysfunctional theirs really was.

By then, we were definitely old enough to know that our mother was no saint. However, we also knew that she was the only mum we had, and so we all decided to gang up against Louis and do whatever we could to make his life uncomfortable. The more tensions grew between them, the more we'd do the things we knew bothered him, like leaving messes around the house, or interrupting important work phone calls he'd take while he was in the house. At the time, I assumed that our stepfather was some kind of successful businessman; even then, I understood that his work must have been lucrative enough to buy the impressive house we lived in. I also figured he'd never really had any exposure to kids, so of course he wouldn't know what to do with us. You can imagine my surprise, then, when I learned later that he not only had kids of his own, but he was actually a family psychologist who taught other parents how to deal with children. That was his *career*, and yet he didn't show even the slightest skill when dealing with me and my siblings. Even as a young child, I could appreciate the irony of that. As time went on, Louis would become a fairly well-known psychologist in Switzerland and France. He even wrote books on the topics he was teaching. One of his more popular books was about how to handle teenagers. It's still often difficult for me to believe, having witnessed firsthand his interactions with us growing up. His books also include a memoir about his life, but there is no mention of us kids or my mum in the whole book. Maybe he knows that time of his life wasn't a prime example for his students.

Despite all of this familial dysfunction, many of my earliest memories were about my attempts to win my mother's attention and affection. There were times of real happiness with her, but in every instance, that joy felt like it came with a catch. She never showed her love easily, if at all. I would always try to do things to bring out the parental love I hoped she had buried inside, even knowing that that love made only the rarest of appearances, and usually at random moments or when I least expected it. Knowing that didn't stop me from forever trying to win her affection, however. For instance, as a little boy, I learned to make coffee on my own and would bring her breakfast in bed. Doing this was the only time I recall receiving recognition for my efforts. She was never big on the good-night kiss, or even an "I love you."

Over time, my constant grab for my mother's love and acceptance slowly shaped me into a person who was always striving to be better and to earn her affection. I figured that, since I was the youngest, the weakest, and the toughest to love,

I needed to work that much harder to be loved by her. I was already convinced that my siblings were better than me in demonstrable ways: Jeffrey was a better runner; Sonia was far more intelligent; Lea was genuinely better at everything else. If I was going to prove that I was worthy of love, I would need to find something to excel at as well. And while I didn't yet know what that thing was, I did know that I didn't want to be just another person. I wanted to be great, even if it would take some time to figure out how. Even at that young age, I knew that the quest for greatness might come at a cost. However, I felt certain I was prepared for whatever that cost might be.

Back then, I also knew there was no point trying to compete with my mum about anything. For as long as I could remember, she had been the most overly confident person I'd ever met. She always insisted that she was *the best* at whatever it was she was doing. Years later, when we'd moved from Switzerland to Australia, we met new friends who invited her to join the church choir for a Christmas concert. After she'd received the invite, she came home to tell us she couldn't possibly accept it.

"I'm not going to sing because I know I'm a good singer," she insisted, as if this explained everything. "I don't want to embarrass the other parents if they're not as good as I am."

"We've never even heard you sing," Sonia replied, saying what we were all thinking.

"You don't need to," she said. "I know I'm good, so I'm not going to perform with them."

As over-the-top as our mum's self-confidence could be, it paled in comparison to her self-righteousness. If she had an idea in her head, or if something made her angry, she stuck to it 100 per cent. Nothing could change her mind, including the truth. If you angered her, that was it, and there was little chance for forgiveness. I don't remember her yelling often, although my sisters insist that she did. What I do recall is the way she would stomp around or give an icy stare that could freeze even the warmest heart. She had an unbelievable ability to hold a grudge; you could feel the bad energy around her, as if it were a dark cloud that blocked out all the sunlight, dropping the temperature from a nice summer day to a freezing winter.

My mum also loved dishing out the silent treatment. She'd think nothing of not talking to us for hours, days—and at one point, *weeks*—even when we were small children. She wouldn't ever explain why she was mad either, so it was a guessing game for us. My siblings would try to have a conversation with her about why she was mad, but she would usually respond with, "You don't know? You're an idiot for not knowing!" There was just no talking to her. It happened so often that amongst ourselves we would say, "Oh, here's another guilt trip coming up. Let's try and figure out what happened this time." She was always making us feel guilty about things we had done.

I am not in contact with my mother today, but from her professional website, I know she's a psychic, a medium, and a Reiki healer (also ironic, I know). If I think back far enough, I recall the introduction of soothing music and incense around our house when she picked up Reiki as a profession. Even more vividly, I remember the arrival of her supposed psychic abilities. Once they appeared, she began making predictions about my whole life and what was going to happen. Most of the time I would listen to her and think, *That's just crazy*. But sometimes those predictions really stung. Often, when I was a child, she'd predict aspects of my future. "You're going to get married twice," she'd say. Or "You're going to lose all your money and then gain it all back again." She'd also say things like, "You will never fly first class, and you will have enough money to buy a Ferrari, but you'll never do it." Telling a child things like that messes with their head. It can make them look for bad things to happen, and then start visualising and believing more good and bad things will come. Even when I was young, I remember deciding that I would never get married—that way, my first marriage couldn't fail. Or I'd decide that I would just head to Las Vegas and get married to some random person for twenty-four hours so that the first marriage was done and over with. I'd also try to account for all the ways I might lose my money and then plan how I could avoid them. It didn't matter that I was years from having a spouse or a job of my own; that's how ingrained those predictions had become in my mind.

Emirates first class 2022.

To this day, I remain envious of people who have close relationships with their parents. No matter how hard I tried, I knew that was never going to be my reality, even though I still held onto a sliver of hope that I could make it happen. I believed that parents were supposed to teach and guide their children. They should show you the right motives and behaviours and inspire you to become your best self. But in our case, my siblings and I were left to figure all of that out on our own.

Sometimes that even meant being literally left on our own.

When I was about nine, my mum went to a hospital near the border of Switzerland and France. She told us she needed surgery and would be gone for about three or four days. Lea was looking after us since our stepdad was no longer in the picture, but she was only about twelve or thirteen. At the time, I thought that situation was fine and normal, but now I realise how utterly wrong (and potentially harmful) it is to leave children at that age unsupervised for days on end. At the time, we had no idea. Without the proper mother and father figures, all four of us were forced to grow up quickly—much quicker than we would have liked. We all learned independence at a young age, and at the cost of a normal childhood.

As I grew older, I began to model my behaviour after what I thought parental figures should do. I assumed that since we didn't have a proper father figure, I could earn acceptance and love by looking after my siblings. I took on that role, hoping I could finally be good at something, or at least feel like I was giving back to my siblings and somehow making their lives better. My way of adopting this role was mostly by listening and observing. I analyzed situations thoroughly and learned when I should—and should not—speak. I learned how to gauge a person's character and what annoyed them, and then I would use those observations to make things work in their favour. I always tried to make other people happy by prioritising them over myself. I became a relationship strategist, able to predict which behaviours would be met well and which would make a situation worse. I also got in the habit of always thinking of the negatives so I could be prepared for the worst-case scenario. At the time, I could have no way of knowing that those skills would one day save my life. All I wanted to do was prove my birth wasn't actually a mistake—and that I had value to offer.

CHAPTER 2

WHEN I WAS TEN, MY MOTHER RELOCATED ME AND MY siblings to Adelaide, Australia. She told us we were moving there to be closer to our father, but as soon as we arrived, my siblings and I knew that wasn't really the case. We might have been closer to my father geographically, but we still didn't have any real relationship with him. For as long as we could remember, our mother had told us biased stories intended to make him look bad in our eyes: he was an alcoholic, a drug user, an all-around bad father. One particular story she liked to tell was that one day when we were young, she came home to find him dangling me by my feet off the third-story apartment unit where we lived. I have no memory of this ever happening, but she swore it was true, saying that it was just another example of him behaving recklessly because he was drunk. Even as a child, I remember thinking that no one would actually do that to a toddler. But my mother told me this story—and others like it—so often that it succeeded in building a negative view of my father in my mind. To this day, my brain can no longer distinguish what my father really did from what my mother *said* he did.

In hindsight, I think our mother was just looking for an excuse to move to Australia so that she could get citizenship there. Saying we'd be close to our dad was the path of least resistance for getting me and my siblings on board. When she first told us about the move, I was excited. We'd already travelled a great deal by then, and I was thinking this would just be a longer version of a cool holiday to a new place. I'd already realised how much I love adventures, and this seemed like a great one. After all, a new environment would bring plenty of new opportunities—maybe even an opportunity for me to finally be worthy of my mother's love.

My first impression of the Australian landscape wasn't positive: the terrain was flat, with red rocks and dead grass everywhere. I missed the mountains, lush green grass, and the alpine lakes of Switzerland. But Australia was also more laid back, easygoing, and stress free. Australia was the cool place to live, and I liked the way everyone seemed so relaxed. Back in Switzerland, there were often television ads for pills to relieve stress and anxiety. In Australia, there was none of that; people just seemed happier and more relaxed there.

Shortly after we arrived in Adelaide, my mother enrolled me and my twin sister, Sonia, at an international school, where we joined kids from Afghanistan, Iraq, Thailand, and a whole heap of other places. I'd always been pretty good at making new friends, and I was excited to have a community beyond our family. On our first day, Sonia and I arrived at the school after classes had already begun. We sat down at our desks and had no idea what the teacher was asking us to do. We'd learned a little bit of English slang in Switzerland, but nowhere near enough of the language to understand what the teacher was saying. I looked around the room, trying to get a sense of what was being asked of us. The other kids were taking out their binders and wrapping their textbooks in protective plastic sleeves. I watched them for a minute or two, studying their movements until I could figure out what we were supposed to be doing. Then I signalled for Sonia to watch, and the two of us began mimicking the other kids.

But that approach only got us so far. When the teacher handed out a sheet of paper with basic prompts like *My name is* _____ or *My age is* _____, Sonia and I knew we'd have to admit we were clueless. Luckily, the teacher was used to kids like us. She came over and helped us work through a few basic English phrases; she also gave us a kids' dictionary to help us translate the words. As it turned out, many of the other kids were in the same boat. We'd all learn a few sentences or new English phrases each day and start incorporating them into our speech. The rest of the time, we spoke a mismatch of words from our own languages, which Sonia and I referred to as *Franglais*. At least my siblings and I had grown up speaking French, which is much closer to English than, say, Arabic or Chinese.

There were plenty of moments with my new schoolmates that were fun. However, I don't think any one of us realised the emotional strain of getting comfortable in a new place, a new culture, and a new language. We were all struggling to adapt to these changes, but no one really talked about it. Instead, that difficulty showed up in the ways we acted towards one another and the short fuses we all seemed to have. One day during recess, I was playing basketball with a boy my age who was much, much smaller. I was guarding him, and no matter how hard he tried, he couldn't get around me. During one point in the game, I reached over his shoulder to grab the ball. He jumped up, and the back of his head hit me square in the mouth, knocking one of my teeth hard enough to kill the root. All the frustration I'd been feeling—the move to a new country, the struggle to learn a new language, my family issues at home—erupted at that moment. I grabbed the basketball from the kid and kicked it as hard as I could. The ball soared up to the roof of the school, where it got stuck. The other boy was furious; I'd taken his ball away and, for all I knew, it could have been the only toy he had. But neither of us really spoke the same language, so we couldn't explain why we were so upset with one another. Instead, he raced after me, scratching his nails down my back and drawing blood, which stained my shirt.

Later that day, the principal called me down to his office. Despite what I had told my teachers about the entire event, it was clear they all thought I was making excuses for kicking the ball. As the principal lectured about what I'd done wrong, I sat down from across his desk but didn't say anything. I wanted to explain what had really happened—about how much it hurt when the kid had whacked me in the mouth and how hard we'd all been trying to find a way to befriend each other in this new setting. But I didn't have the words for any of that, so all the principal knew was that I'd kicked another kid's ball onto the roof of the school. I was sure I was going to be suspended for it. But then my mother came to pick me up. She asked what had happened, and I told her. I couldn't believe what happened next: she actually defended me that day, explaining to the principal about how the kid had whacked me in the face and left huge scratches down my back. For once, she was acting like a proper mum.

When the principal still seemed sceptical about my story, my mother asked me to stand up and show him the scratches on my back. I could see the disbelief on the principal's face: I *had* been telling the truth, at least as best as I could in this new language.

"Wow, okay," he said. "You can go back to your class."

For a moment, I felt vindicated and triumphant. I had been so angry when the teachers hadn't believed my story. I had told the truth all along, and it bothered me that they hadn't seen that. As far as I was concerned, this had already become a pattern in my world. Adults were all the same—they didn't believe me, and talking to them would just make me feel more helpless and hopeless. Nevertheless, I still felt like I had to prove them wrong. But all that vindication I felt evaporated when I learned that the principal had decided to send the other boy home. Now I was the one getting a kid in trouble for no reason. The whole incident had started when I was standing over the guy, guarding him. Sure, it had gotten out of hand, but that wasn't really anyone's fault. I didn't want this kid to get suspended any more than I wanted to be in trouble myself. Even at that age, I understood the consequences of snitching on someone. I'd done damage I never intended, both by robbing the kid of what might have been the one toy he was given that whole year and now also the chance to be in school with the rest of us. For all I knew, he came from a poor family that could barely afford to send him to school, let alone buy him a new ball. Now, on top of that, he might get in trouble with his parents, all because we both overreacted to a game. It was the first real lesson I had in the power of speech and the way our words can hurt people, whether we mean them to or not.

No matter how hard school or my family relationships seemed, I could always count on the excitement of a holiday trip to lift my spirits. While the parents of my classmates were buying new cars or bigger houses, my mother was always saving her money for our next adventure. My siblings and I loved to travel, whether it was going back to Europe for the summer or driving around the Australian outback. A year after we arrived in Australia, my mother announced that we were taking a road trip to Flinders Ranges, the largest mountain chain in South Australia. She probably thought it would remind us of everything we loved about the Swiss Alps, although the highest peak in the Flinders Ranges is 1,171 metres, which is around the same size as the average hill in Switzerland. But that didn't matter; we would still have the chance to explore a new place.

The trip to the mountains took five hours. We didn't have to get too far outside of Adelaide before we saw our first wild Australian animals: kangaroos, dingoes, camels, and emus. It was totally mind-blowing for four Swiss kids. Before long, we began seeing kangaroos everywhere. We began a game counting the number of roadkill kangaroos we passed and got up to 150 in no time. They were so common you didn't even have to try, and so the game quickly became boring. By then, we still had hours to go on the drive. We probably complained. I'm sure that irritated our mother.

After we arrived at the Flinders Ranges, she checked us into our accommodations, which was a little container house called a *donga*. We began getting ready for dinner at sunset. The horizon was amazing: pinks and oranges, like the whole sky was on fire. We were surrounded by a desert landscape marked by weathered fences. Dozens of kangaroos hopped around the site, and we had fun watching them move around. Eventually, my family and I sat down at a wooden picnic table, and we started snacking on chips as we watched the scenery. As far as we kids were concerned, everything was great. But then, without saying a word, our mum stood up and stomped into our rented accommodation. We had no idea why, but we could tell she wasn't happy. The next thing we knew, she came out with a suitcase in her hand. By that time, the sun had set, so we got up from the table to see what was going on.

"Pack your things and get in the car," she told us.

"But we paid for the night," responded one of my sisters.

"Yeah," said my mom. "And now we're leaving."

We packed our luggage and got into the car. Our mother began driving without saying a word. None of us knew what was going on. Someone tried to ask, but she was giving us the silent treatment. It was incredibly awkward. My older brother was in the front passenger seat; my two sisters and I were in the back. We were all frightened and unsure of what was going on. Sure, we'd gotten bored and grumpy on the drive to the mountains, but could that really be the reason?

Our mother never said a word. Instead, she kept driving until she got tired. By then, we had left the dirt road to our camp and were on a two-lane highway with no real shoulder. She pulled over to one side so we could nap, but we were still dangerously close to the road trains roaring by, each with multiple trailers in tow. The rigs were huge, some pulling as many as seven trailers—dozens of massive wheels careening just centimetres from our car. Each time one passed by, our vehicle would shake. We were still in the desert, and with the car turned off, the interior also became unbearably hot. Eventually, my brother opened his door. As he did, a rush of cool air came into the car. My sisters and I sighed a collective, silent sigh of relief. But at the same time my brother opened the door, the dome light came on and the car began to beep. My mother awoke and flew into a rage.

"It's so hot," my brother Jeffrey insisted. "What the hell do you want us to do?"

He tried putting his finger on the door sensor to stop the beeping. The noise ceased, but our mum was still angry. Every little sound was setting her off—so much so that my sister was even afraid to grab her water bottle from the driver's seat back pocket for fear that it would make our mother even more mad. I knew not to say a word to my mother at that moment. Even the thought of speaking to her gave me the chills and the shakes. I was scared of what she would say and do if I tried to speak. I didn't want to be in trouble with her, and I didn't want to make her more angry. I could feel the adrenaline coursing through my body. I was just eleven years old and yet was already so afraid of her. Instead of saying anything, I tried to make sense of the situation: *I don't understand*, I thought to myself. *We had an accommodation booked. Why would you decide to leave and sleep on the side of the highway with four kids in the car?*

It didn't make sense at all. And even at that age, I knew our predicament was super dangerous. The only reason I could come up with was that we had so disappointed our mother that she couldn't bear to be on holiday with us. I decided that the real lesson of the day was that I had somehow failed our mum. I was a disappointment to her and needed to do better. It was a belief I had already begun to internalise, but now those feelings had crystallised and would define all of my interactions with our mother or anyone else from that moment forward. I was certain that if I could just be better, just climb my way up onto a pedestal, she would finally approve of me and be happy.

I kept believing that until I was fifteen. That summer, we visited Sion, an ancient Swiss city near the German border. While we were there, we rented a huge chalet at the end of a single one-way road, deep in the forest. From our chalet, the next nearest town was Nax, a small village of maybe two hundred people, which reminded me of Vésenaz. When I was a kid, Vésenaz was my whole world, so it made Nax feel all the more special, what with its snowcapped mountains and gorgeous views. From the chalet, we could see both the surrounding forest and the stunning mountains. Nearby were similar wooden houses and a recreational soccer field. It was a kid's dream—absolutely stunning. The soccer field was full sized and almost the only flat area around. Seeing how none of the other nearby villages had a field, I imagined this was where all the soccer tournaments took place for local teams. The soccer field itself was flanked by a walk that led to a lookout point and a large wooden cross. While I played on the field, dribbling a ball and hoping other kids would show up and want to play, my mother would walk to the cross and back. It seemed like, just maybe, she was having a good time and that this would be a smooth trip.

I had always been fascinated with medieval history, and the Sion region is filled with it. The thought of enacting childhood dreams of castles and knights kept me excited for the entire trip. In the town of Sion itself, two dramatic hills rise out of nowhere. On one is a huge old cathedral built in the sixth century AD. Across from it sits a medieval castle with stone towers, sentry walks, and turreted fortification walls. It really was like something out of a fairy tale. The hill leading up to the castle was rugged and steep—about two hundred metres high. Getting to the top was quite a trek, but we had hiked it before, and my mother was convinced we should do it again.

It was already hot and sunny when she, Sonia, and I began the climb. We didn't get very far before flies began buzzing all around us. My twin sister and I started complaining. By the time we reached the top, our mum was furious. She stormed off ahead of us, and no matter how hard we tried, we couldn't catch up. Eventually, we lost her in the crowd, so we decided to go back down the hill and wait for her at the large open area separating the two landmarks. As our mum approached, I could see she was still mad. I thought about all the hikes we'd taken when I was younger—how Sonia and I would pretend that we lived outside a medieval castle not unlike this one. I'd always imagined myself as the humble young man who was willing and eager to help or even save the day. I fantasised that I would be the one who would leap up to save an injured rider thrown from a horse, only to discover later that he was actually a prince. Those dreams had made me feel brave and important. I loved believing that I was the person who would always protect people who couldn't protect themselves.

I knew that Sonia was at least as brave as I was. I also knew she was probably even better at protecting herself from our mum than I was. But something in that situation made me want to be the one protecting her. I was too nervous to stand up to our mother with words, so instead, as she approached us, I let out a long whistle—the kind of whistle a kid testing boundaries would try. I meant it to say, *What the hell? Why are you storming past us?* As soon as I saw her face, I knew whistling was a huge mistake. Her eyes grew dark, and white-hot anger radiated out of her.

"What's wrong?" I asked our mother.

That was also definitely the wrong thing to do. She whipped around to face me and Sonia.

"You're ungrateful, and you've already complained way too much on this holiday," she hissed. "I should send you both back to Australia."

She kept yelling, saying all kinds of hurtful things I've since blocked out of my memory. But the details don't really matter. It was just like the trip to Flinders Ranges; as far as she was concerned, we were ungrateful. A disappointment. We had failed her.

Eventually, our mother stormed off again. We followed her all the way back to the car park. She sat briefly on a bench on the nearby sidewalk, where she continued to berate us. An older gentleman sat not too far from us, and he looked at me and Sonia with pity in his eyes. My mother eventually got back into the car. We followed her there. She told us again how ungrateful we were and how tempted she was to send us back home.

"I just need some time away from you," she concluded as she started the car.

It was Sonia who first realised how serious our mother was about driving away.

"I've got my wallet in your bag," Sonia told her. "Can I have it, please?"

This wasn't the first time our mother had abruptly left my sister. Without some money, Sonia knew there'd be nothing we could do until our mother decided to return. Later, Sonia would tell me that she was actually trying to protect me; she knew it was the first time I'd been left like this by our mother, and she wanted to make it easier on me.

"At least if we had money, we could have had some fun," Sonia explained to me. "We could have gone to the cafeteria and gotten a hot chocolate or seen a movie or wandered around the gift shop until mum's emotions calmed down a little bit and she mellowed out."

We were barely teenagers, but my sister had already figured out this was the only way to deal with our mother's rages.

After she drove away, our mother stayed missing for hours. The older gentleman who'd witnessed it all continued to watch us. I can't remember if he said or did anything, but looking back I wonder what I would have done in his position. Would I have interfered? Should he have? I'm still not sure.

With our mum long gone, Sonia and I walked around and tried to entertain ourselves. When that didn't work, we began strategising about how to get out of this predicament. We were too far from the chalet to walk back, and even if we could, we had no idea if we'd even find our belongings there when we arrived. By that point in my life, I'd begun working part-time jobs, so I had a little money saved up. Maybe I could buy a plane ticket back to Australia. I imagined myself arriving at the ticket counter and the way the staff would take extra care to help me get through security and eventually onto the plane, simply because I was a minor. The flight attendants would pay close attention to me, always making sure I felt comfortable and safe. *This won't be so bad,* I told myself. *It'll actually be kind of cool.*

I was dreaming about a world in which I could be by myself on a fun adventure. In that fantasy, I could succeed in pretending that our mum wasn't actually our biological mother but rather a stranger whose duty was to look after us. Clearly, she was bad at her job. So of course I could just pick her up and leave her whenever I wanted.

I was still imagining how I'd get off the plane and call a mate's mum to pick me up from the airport when our mother pulled up in her rental car, finally ready to take us home.

Back at the chalet, she praised Sonia for the way she'd behaved.

"You've done nothing wrong," our mother told Sonia. "It was Alex who was angry at me. He caused this whole issue."

That was a turning point in our relationship. It would be years before I'd hear the psychological term *gaslighting*, but even then, I knew what our mother was doing was wrong. She'd stormed away from us in a strange place. She'd yelled and screamed in public. She'd driven away from her two young children and left them to fend for themselves. I'd seen her do this kind of postmortem blaming after an event before. I'd watched how she would choose one of us to blame while telling the others it was that first child's fault.

The next morning, my mother asked me if I was still angry with her.

"Yes," I said. "Obviously. You left us."

"In that case, you can stay here," she told me.

She and Sonia left for another hike without me. While they were gone, I spent the day looking at one-way flights to Australia. When they finally returned, Sonia took me aside. We both agreed the only way to save the trip was for me to apologise.

"I'm sorry for whistling at you," I told my mother. "I'm sorry for complaining about the flies. I'll stop being ungrateful. I promise."

I was back to believing that if I could just be better, I could stop my mother from being so angry. And in that instance, I guess it worked, which is to say that she didn't cancel the rest of our holiday. But the entire incident had put another wedge between me and my mother that would never go away. I'd tried to stand up to her, to keep me and Sonia safe. But instead of realising that, our mother only saw an ungrateful child who needed to be punished. I'd spent fifteen years trying to overcome being the youngest sibling and weakest member of our family. I knew I couldn't beat Sonia at schoolwork. I couldn't beat our older siblings at running or sports or anything else. But I could be the brave one, the kid who was willing to take a stand, no matter how scary that felt—except even doing that wasn't enough to earn our mother's love or approval. I knew it was wrong of her to leave us in a town we didn't know, a place where we barely spoke the language. That was no way for a proper parent to behave.

What I didn't know was that her behaviour was about to get much worse.

Back in Australia, our mother's relationship with my brother, Jeffrey, continued to deteriorate. By that time, he was seventeen and prone to emotional outbursts. My mum always liked to say my older siblings were experiencing an adolescent crisis and that those kinds of outbursts were just them being normal teenagers, growing up and defying their parents. She'd warn Sonia and me against going through that phase, telling us that our siblings' defiant behaviour was what kept them home while we twins were taken on holidays. If only Jeffrey and Lea had behaved better and been kinder to her, they would have been able to go, too.

Truthfully, what was happening with Jeffrey seemed to me much more than just an adolescent crisis. Because my sisters and I had good social skills, we made friends easily and could spend lots of time out of the house. But Jeffrey had never really learned how to socialise. I realise now how trapped he must have felt and how much he must have been suffering. Jeffrey spent most of his time in his room. I could tell that he was growing more and more frustrated and angry. He knew that he was too tall and too strong to be restrained by my mother's words or her instructions. Nothing seemed to contain him anymore. My mother, meanwhile, hadn't relinquished any of her need to be controlling: everything *she* said was correct; everything *we* said was wrong.

I don't remember what, exactly, caused their growing tension to explode. Probably my mother was yelling about something and making Jeffrey feel even worse about his own difficulties. What I do remember is one dinner when he picked up his plate and smashed it on the table. At that point, my sisters and I would have done anything to get away from the scene. Maybe we tried to clean up the kitchen; maybe my mum sent us to our rooms. I don't remember that either. But I do know that, in the days that followed, Jeffrey disappeared. At some point later that same day, my mum approached me while I was sitting on the living room couch.

"The police were called," she told me. "Jeffrey was taken away."

Apparently, she'd arranged for him to go to a home for troubled kids. But before she could explain what had happened to my brother, she instead launched into one of her pity pleas. She complained about how Jeffrey had overreacted with the plate and how difficult he had become. She brought back up all the complaints she'd been harbouring from the past. She had all kinds of excuses about why Jeffrey's behaviour wasn't her fault and how hurtful and inappropriate it was for him to call her a terrible parent.

I disagreed.

"You kicked him out," I challenged. "You called the cops."

This wasn't like me—standing up to her like that. But I had had enough. My brother deserved to be defended. And so I lobbed the biggest verbal punch I could.

"After all that you've done to him, why wouldn't Jeffrey feel that way about you?" I demanded.

My mother must have been shocked at first. But that disbelief quickly changed to anger when she realised I wasn't about to go along with her version of events. She stormed towards me. And then she slapped me.

Of course I was upset, and I'm sure it showed. She tried to apologise, but it was in one of her backhanded ways.

"I'm sorry I hit you," she began. "But you shouldn't have said what you said. It wasn't nice."

She tried to smile and give me a pat on the head as if to say that everything would be all right.

I knew it wouldn't be.

Afterwards, I probably went to my room and cried from the surprise and sadness of being hit. However, that sadness was soon replaced with a weird sense of relief. At least this time,

I knew why my mother was mad at me. There was no silent treatment, no guessing what I had done to disappoint her, no need to conference with my siblings to see if they knew what offense I had committed. I'd tried to defend my brother, just like I had tried to defend my twin sister back in Switzerland. In the past, when I'd tried to stand up to my mum, her resulting anger would leave me feeling awful. I'd withdraw, knowing I was in trouble and trying to figure out how I could do better next time—how I could make her like me again. I'd analyze the situation, trying to pinpoint where I had messed up and how I could avoid that mistake in the future. But this time I knew what I'd done. And I wasn't even sure I was sorry.

I had already missed out on important parts of a healthy childhood. Not feeling loved or understood by my mother had forced me to grow up far too soon. I'd never really had the opportunity to act as a child or to enjoy youth. The littlest things a child could find joy in, like Christmas celebrations, were even taken away from us. After that Christmas with the helicopter back in Switzerland, I couldn't remember another holiday celebration spent as a family—no tree, no decorations, none of it. My mum would often take us on holidays in lieu of celebrating, but what would have been the harm in decorating the house ahead of time, to get us kids happy and excited? Some years, I'd go to a shopping centre and buy tinsel for myself then put it around my bedroom. It was the only holiday spirit I experienced at home.

Most importantly, I still had no idea what parental love felt like, which also meant I had no idea how to experience love between friends or young romantic love either. My siblings and I lived in a kind of survival mode, where we were totally focused on enduring our childhoods rather than receiving positive emotions and a sense of connection. Even though they tried, our friends' parents couldn't compensate either. I knew their affection wasn't the same as a parent's for their child. Instead, it felt like pity. I wanted real love, the kind you read about or see in movies—that spark and glow when two people really care about each other. Instead, all I had come to feel was a dark, suffocating presence in my heart. *If my own mother couldn't love me, then how could anyone else? How could I?*

I couldn't possibly have known it at the time, but I was already experiencing classic symptoms of post-traumatic stress disorder. I had no one to guide me through it. By high school, I didn't have a relationship with our father at all. My brother was gone. My lingering Swiss accent meant that I was getting bullied at school. Unconsciously, I began seeking out mates who seemed to have experienced the same kind of trauma. I also looked for those kids whom I felt would accept me and all my flaws. Some of these new friends had also never experienced proper parenting, so they thought nothing of rebelling every chance they got. We hung out at houses where the parents couldn't care less what we were up to. We drank. We tried drugs. Deep down, I knew that none of this was a good idea. But I was so glad to finally have a circle of friends that I went along with whatever they suggested.

My sisters watched all of this unfold. Occasionally, they'd complain about what some of my female friends were wearing or about their hair and makeup. When they did, I'd agree that I shouldn't hang out with these friends anymore. I wasn't about to do anything to lose my bond with my sisters. I had to please them; if they were at least happy, then maybe I could be happy, too. I clung to a sliver of hope that maybe—*just maybe*—we could have a happy family household. But the truth of the matter was that my sisters were dealing with far too much of their own emotional fallout from our mother to actually feel happy or to really care about my well-being as a rebelling teenager.

Without that familial affirmation, the only comfort I had left was food. So I started eating. A lot. Each day after school, I'd come home and eat a bag of chips while playing video games. Whenever I had money, I'd cook huge dinners for myself. I began gaining weight, which only made me feel worse. What I didn't realise at the time was that I was trying to self-soothe the only way I knew how. While other kids had learned to calm themselves with affection from their parents and the knowledge that they were secure in their relationships and attachments, I'd had none of that. So instead, I was relying on the chemicals released in the brain when we eat junk food, hoping they'd make me feel like I was loved—or that they would at least distract me from my pain and loneliness. It would take years before I understood the brain science behind those choices—and just how many people resort to similar coping mechanisms. At the time, I knew I was experiencing a terrible feeling of emptiness I would have done almost anything to fill.

CHAPTER 3

BY THE TIME I GRADUATED HIGH SCHOOL, MY RELATIONship with my mother had deteriorated even further. Eventually, it seemed to disintegrate altogether. Although we shared the same DNA, she was not my parent in any real sense. Instead, she'd become a complete stranger—and a hostile one at that. I'd intuited that these beliefs were true for some time; they were all confirmed the day my mother threw me out of the house.

That final explosion occurred not long before my eighteenth birthday. By then, Sonia was off travelling in Europe for a gap year and Lea had moved back to Switzerland, so it was just me and our mum in the house. I'd been working at a local discount store called The Warehouse. My days were extremely long. I'd go from a full day at school to an eight-hour shift at The Warehouse. One day after work, I arrived home to find my mattress on the floor, my laptop taken from its usual setup on my desk, and all my clothes removed from my wardrobe.

"What's going on?" I asked my mum, concerned. "What happened in my bedroom?"

"You'll be eighteen soon," she said, without a hint of regret. "You're pretty much an adult. I'm leaving Australia in a month, so you're on your own. You need to get out of the house."

I was incredulous. "You're leaving Australia? When did this happen? Where are you going?"

Despite my questioning, she didn't have much else to say. She'd made up her mind. She was heading off somewhere I can't even recall (or perhaps have chosen not to remember), supposedly to further her Reiki practice. I was to be left behind.

To be honest, I wasn't entirely surprised that she was kicking me out.

When my mum kicked out Jeffrey, part of me knew the rest of us would eventually meet a similar fate. Life with her had alternated between living with a ticking time bomb on the one hand and an emotional prison sentence on the other. Once Jeffrey was gone, I'd deliberately started spending less and less time at home. Lea moved out not long after. Meanwhile, Sonia and I silently prepared ourselves for the inevitable.

But even knowing this moment was coming, it still shocked me to the core. Our mother had given me no notice of my impending eviction, no time to find other lodging or to psychologically prepare for being on my own. I felt devastated—and more alone than ever. That night, I cried myself to sleep on my mattress. As I began to drift off, I could hear my mum yelling from the other room.

"You can't just stay there and cry all night!" she shouted.

That made me sob even more.

With few housing options available to me, I decided to call my friend Nick, whose parents, Denise and Michael, were wonderful and kind. I asked if I could stay with them in the short term. I'd gotten close with Nick's parents by then—having bonded with them in place of having my own parents—so I knew they'd be happy to take me in for a few days. Before any of us had a chance to commit, though, I realised the approach Denise and Michael would likely take. They were already aware of the ongoing drama with my family, and I knew I'd be flooded with questions now that things had officially come to a head. I wanted time to work things out on my own before I tried to explain them to anyone else. So, instead, I called another friend, Riley. He had dealt with his share of family troubles, too. I figured if I could stay with him, I'd dodge at least some of the questions I'd receive from Denise and Michael. Riley's mother agreed to house me for a few days and actually came to pick me up within fifteen or twenty minutes of me making the call.

The next day I went back to my house for the last time and packed everything I owned into some sports bags, backpacks, and a few trash bags. I had decided to take everything with me, including the mattress and anything in that house I considered mine. As I prepared to leave, however, I discovered there was one more argument left to have.

"You're not taking that mattress!" my mum yelled. "I paid for that! Either bring that mattress back or give me one hundred dollars."

I don't remember exactly what else she said at that moment. All I know is I screamed back like I'd never screamed before. When we were younger, she'd told me and my siblings that her parents had been terrible. In that final argument, I used that revelation as ammunition.

"You are as bad as your own parents!" I shouted. I hadn't known them personally, but I knew that comment would cut deep. "If you ever want to speak to me again, you're going to have to apologise for everything you did to us kids," I concluded as I stormed out of the house.

After that, my mind went blank. I was shaking, my vision was blurred, and a massive hot flash engulfed my entire body. I knew I didn't want to be near my mum at that moment, or ever again for that matter. For a while after that, I remember thinking that if I found out by chance she had died, I'd feel no emotion about it at all.

Staying with Riley's family turned out to be short lived. One of my first nights there, I cried myself to sleep thinking about how much of a failure I was and how pathetic I must be in my mother's eyes. And then Riley's mum said the same thing mine had said only a couple of days earlier: "You can't just stay there and cry all night." That made me angry—on top of feeling uncontrollably sad. I figured if I couldn't even be vulnerable there, where *could* I be vulnerable? I decided I needed my own place, and I needed it quickly. I wanted to block my mum out of my mind completely. I just wanted to *forget*.

Luckily, I quickly found some roommates: people around my age whom I'd met through an online ad for house shares. I loved their house. It was modern, maybe only two years old at the time, and single story. Located in a new suburban estate, it didn't have many other homes around. Instead, we were surrounded by tons of open land, including a dense forest and rocky creek bed. I got along well with my new roommates, and I finally felt a weight lifted off my shoulders, knowing I could wake up each day without constant stress hanging overhead.

As shocked as I initially felt about my eviction from my own home, I also began to take pride in my newfound independence. I had a job and a place to call my own. I felt like a responsible adult rather than a worthless child living under an unloving mother's roof.

That newfound self-possession motivated me. I took a second job at an events planning company, where we organised parties for high-profile people like Steve Irwin's daughter, Bindi. I felt proud that I could fully support myself and take care of my own needs. As the emotional weight of life with my mother began to lift, I began to look for ways to improve other aspects of my life as well. I stopped using food as an emotional aid, and I made a commitment to drop the weight I'd gained. I started running every day, often in the forest near our house. I also changed my diet and stuck to it: I'd have a meal replacement shake in the morning; a salad for lunch; and something like steak, eggs, and a vegetable for dinner. I kept at it, and within three months, I lost thirty kilos.

Life went on nicely like this for a couple of years. However, although I was somewhat happy, I also kept thinking I could do more. Yes, my life was good, but couldn't it be better? I'd never abandoned those desires to be a hero and save someone in distress. And as much as I hoped to forget her, thoughts of my mum lingered. I'd imagine accomplishing something really big in life and how she'd find out and finally call to tell me how proud she was. It angered me to know I still held onto that hope, but that anger didn't prevent those thoughts from occurring.

The fact is, I still wanted the chance to prove I could be great. And the easiest way to do that seemed to be joining the military. In Switzerland, serving in the military is required by law, so for me it felt like a natural progression. I still had a Swiss passport, but when I looked into joining their forces, there were some challenges, including a language barrier with the Swiss German training camp I'd have to attend (I didn't speak a bit of German). However, I'd already become fully committed to the idea of enlisting, so I decided to sign a one-year contract as a driver for the Australian military. Once I made that decision, I felt an immediate sense of pride in the idea of serving my country. That feeling alone made me certain I'd chosen correctly.

My basic training was set to take place in Kapooka, a suburban town in New South Wales and home to the Australian Department of Defense's Army Recruit Training Centre. Before I even arrived there, I had my first lesson about what life in the military would really be like. Prior to training school, new recruits were required to pass a series of fitness tests. The tests were pretty simple: push-ups and sit-ups, some running, that sort of thing. All of my recent physical conditioning paid off, and I passed the tests easily. At the end of the day, the Personal Training Instructors (PTIs) asked us to pick up the mats and cones we'd used throughout the day. I did as I was told. One of the PTIs thanked me on the way out and wished me the best of luck.

As I was walking out, I noticed other guys around me hadn't followed the instructions to tidy up.

"How useless do you want to be?!" I heard a PTI screaming at the guys. "If you can't even follow simple instructions now, how the hell do you think you're going to be in Kapooka?"

I knew then that I'd need to take everything they said seriously. Right then and there, I committed to being the best recruit I could be.

By this point, Nick's family had become a surrogate family for me. When it was time to leave for Kapooka, his father, Michael, saw me off. This was a big moment in my life, and it meant a great deal to have a father figure there to share it with me.

"We're proud of you, Alex," Michael said before I got onto the bus. That word *proud* stopped me in my tracks. So did what he said next: "I know it's tough for you to hear, but there are a lot of people who are proud. I'm just one of them."

I couldn't manage any words in return. Instead, I just smiled through a clenched jaw, tensing all the muscles in my face in an effort to hold back my tears. I felt overwhelmed with emotion, but I didn't want to cry in front of the group of people I'd be training and living with for the next eighty days. Michael's words touched something deep within me. I felt appreciated in a way I never had before, and his compliment was what I'd hoped for for so much of my life up until that point.

After our goodbyes, I boarded the bus and we were off to the airport. We flew from Brisbane to Sydney, then in Sydney we got on another bus to Kapooka. As we entered the training facility, everything became very real: the firing ranges and obstacle courses, the barracks, the precision with which people in uniform moved around campus. They were soldiers. Would I ever measure up?

I didn't have long to think about that question. As soon as the bus came to a stop, an officer instructed us to assemble in a large room. There, we sat down for a roll call and then were ordered to line up. We were next told which platoon and class we'd be in. Then an officer asked me for my home address.

"I don't have one," I replied. I wasn't lying. I'd moved out of the house where I'd been living, and I was carrying nearly everything I owned in the bags I'd brought to Kapooka.

"Well, where are your parents located?" the officer asked.

"I don't talk to them," I said, then paused for a second. "I don't have parents."

"Well, we have to have an address for you somewhere in here. We need a location to send your mail."

I had to think about it for a minute before responding, "OK, here is Denise and Michael's address."

That moment solidified for me just how high the stakes had become. I needed to succeed at Kapooka; it was my last hope. I had nowhere else to go, so I'd have to make the military work. I would stay and try my hardest, no matter what was thrown at me.

It didn't take long at Kapooka for me to realise how much I liked the way the military taught us. I liked getting a specific order, to be somewhere at a certain time, and having to follow it. I knew if we broke their simple rules, we'd be reprimanded, even for something as simple as being a few minutes late. I didn't want to get yelled at if I could avoid it, so I did everything I could to follow each and every rule. If I ever messed up, I took it as a lesson that I needed to think quicker, be better at resolving problems, or learn to move more efficiently. I started listening to every word of every instruction so I always, *always* knew what was expected of me. The years I'd spent as a child searching for reasons my mum was mad and constantly having to guess where I stood were slowly being put to bed by this new, straightforward way of existing. It was easy for me to follow the rules if I knew what they were.

Some of the training at Kapooka was basic care, like getting ready quickly. At the beginning, our sergeants gave us ten minutes to make our beds, shower, shave, get dressed, and complete whatever other task they had for us. Then, over time, they'd lessen the amount of time we had to complete the same set of tasks, until ultimately it was down to a six-minute time limit. We'd be able to do it because we were always picking up new tricks about how to do things better and quicker. In many ways, the training felt like a game, and that made it easier to follow. Some of the other guys would get angry and complain about what seemed like a bunch of senseless orders. But I knew it was all part of the training: we just had to play along, no matter the cost. One of our daily exercises was marching in a parade formation, where we had to walk in sync wearing special parade shoes; mine ended up taking off three layers of skin because they were pressing against my heel so much. The medic told me to stop parading, but I couldn't. I didn't want to get backtracked from everyone else in training. So, I put on some Band-Aids and multiple layers of socks and kept enduring.

Much to my relief, most of the training at Kapooka felt manageable. Going in, I had assumed that I would struggle with the physical training, but happily that wasn't the case. In fact, the most challenging part of Kapooka for me turned out to be the weapons training. I hadn't grown up around guns at all. I had no idea how to use them, so it took me a while to catch on. Once I did, I began to enjoy even some of the most intense weapons instruction. Towards the end of basic training, we had an obstacle course where we had to first fix a bayonet onto an assault rifle and then run through trenches and water to attack a sandbagged target. We also had to jump through and over all kinds of crazy obstacles. It was much like what I'd seen in the movies, and it was actually a lot of fun.

All the guys at Kapooka became quick friends because we all pushed each other to do our best. If someone was struggling with push-ups, we'd stand by his side and count them out to keep him accountable. When I encountered difficulties mastering weapons, my mates would help me understand how to clean, load, and handle them. We were always looking out for each other. It was the real definition of camaraderie. I'd consider that the main thing I learned from Kapooka—that and how to think quickly, no matter the crisis.

Portrait of me during Kapooka.

After our eighty-day training, those who remained were ready to graduate. Nick and Michael had promised to attend; however, one of their flights was delayed, so they couldn't make it. Finding out that they wouldn't be able to attend was a real blow. Until that moment, I don't think I realised how much I was looking forward to seeing them; it would have been the first time anyone other than my siblings had flown to see me anywhere. Hearing they couldn't make it crushed me. I found solace in knowing that Sonia would be there. Marching out with my fellow trainees and knowing we were now all soldiers made me feel proud, and I was glad Sonia could witness it. I still have a photo of us from that day. We were both so happy, and I could tell that she was proud of me.

After Kapooka, I was sent to Initial Employment Training (IET), which took place in Victoria. I'd become a private, or entry-level soldier, and it was time to learn my specific job. I was tasked with becoming a driver, which meant I would have to learn how to operate trucks and other military vehicles. Once I'd mastered those basic skills, I was assigned my official military unit: 1 RAR (Royal Australian Regiment). I also learned that I would be based in Townsville, Northern Queensland.

While I was at IET, I made several lifelong friends: Amber, Pete, and Tobi, who were also assigned to the 1 RAR. Blond, fit, and good-looking, Tobi is the kind of guy people want to be around. He has a loud, distinctive laugh and is often the life of the party. In many ways, he and I are total opposites. He's full of confidence—a cocky guy who is so much fun to be around and who always seems happy to go with the flow. I, on the other hand, am more like the responsible dad of any crew.

Tobi and me, pre-Caribbean cruise.

Amber and me in Switzerland.

At IET, most of our gang were younger than I, and they could also be incredibly immature. Initially, I always refused when they asked me to go out with them. Eventually, they persuaded me. In hindsight, I'm grateful they did; those nights out with my new mates helped me become less uptight and stressed all the time. Tobi, especially, taught me a lot about how to relax and be happy in the moment.

Townsville's climate was a shock to my system—as hot and humid as any tropical destination. After spending most of my life in the mountains and dry fresh air, it felt suffocating there. Initially, I was miserable and regretted my posting. But in time, I came to love it. While it wouldn't be the most fulfilling or challenging work of my life, it was the best fun a twenty-something young Aussie could have. Each morning, we awoke at six o'clock and got ready for the day. Then it was an hour or so of physical training, followed by breakfast and whatever job we'd been assigned. We'd get an hour lunch break, and then if we'd finished our work, we could all go as a group to the gym or play indoor soccer until calling it a day. After work on Fridays, we'd head back to our air-conditioned rooms, which were usually soaked with condensation because of the humidity. But we didn't care. It felt great to be in the cold air, and we'd relax in front of videos or play some songs on YouTube. Then, we'd start drinking and have a barbecue. I loved the structure of the week and the chance to hang out and have fun with friends. During our downtime, I began mountain biking and trail running, and Tobi would join me whenever he wasn't busy trying to flirt with whatever new woman had caught his eye.

Tobi and me watching Tomorrowland aftermovie in my room on Base in Townsville.

A few years into our time at Townsville, we were informed we might be deployed to Afghanistan. Our training for that deployment began immediately, and I embraced it with real enthusiasm. My favorite part was the Helicopter Underwater Escape Training (HUET): basically, a model helicopter built to scale and suspended above a pool. Trainees are strapped in and blindfolded, then the simulator helicopter crashes into the water and spins upside down. Without taking off your blindfold, you have to figure out how to get out of your seat belt, open the window, and swim to the surface, all the while making sure there's no oil or fuel there that could ignite and burn you alive. It may sound crazy, but I liked the HUET so much that I redid it two or three times, just for fun. We were also given medical training and taught how to rescue someone from a vehicle. To many civilians, the training might seem gruesome. In one case, for instance, we weren't told that the practice dummy had had his legs amputated by the pretend crash; when I tried to lift him over my shoulder, his legs came off, squirting fake blood everywhere. It was awful, but I also knew they were trying to prepare us for the realities of war.

I had no idea when or where in Afghanistan I would be deployed, but in a way, it didn't matter; that training was worth it, no matter how hard it may have been at the time. The things we learned were invaluable, and I knew they could save my life.

In the Australian military, soldiers have a choice whether they want to accept a deployment or not. I knew a few guys who had refused theirs. I, on the other hand, saw it as the pinnacle of my career. When my opportunity came to go to Afghanistan, I jumped at it. Boarding the first plane that would take me there didn't feel all that different than going on a holiday. By then, I had already travelled to nearly fifty countries. The only obvious difference now was that we were all in uniform.

Our first stop was in Darwin. Then we flew to Dubai, the Middle Eastern hub for the Australian military. There, we were given our assault rifles. We also spent a week acclimatising at a camp and preparing for what might await us in Afghanistan. Things definitely began to feel real there.

"It's not like you're walking the streets of Australia now," one officer warned us. "You need to carry an assault rifle that's loaded and ready to go all the time."

When we landed in Kabul, one of the first things I saw was Camp KAIA, a massive international installation. I was shocked to see how different it was from the military bases back in Australia. KAIA wasn't just huge, it also had amenities like volleyball courts and restaurants. It was a lot more than any of us expected to see in a military camp, especially one in a war-torn country.

We weren't there long before we were off to Camp KARGA,

where we would spend the next seven months. Camp KARGA was small in comparison, and we had some Americans and some United Kingdom personnel there as well. I was a little surprised to learn that many people on our deployment had never travelled to the Middle East before. I had some understanding of Middle Eastern culture and religions from holidays in Jordan and Israel, but many people I was with knew very little about this culture. Prior to our deployment, the Australian military had required us to take a course or two intended to educate us on Afghani culture, but that education was by no means extensive. And although those classes covered the basics like traditional customs, clothing, and cuisine, I'd already learned from my own travels that you really have to experience those elements firsthand to understand. As I would soon learn, what we probably most needed was a crash course in what the roads were going to be like, what we could expect to see and experience along the way, and what activities or celebrations should be considered dangerous. As it turned out, most deployed soldiers had to learn that kind of thing the hard way.

When my military unit arrived at Camp KARGA, the mission there was in the process of being converted into one of peacekeeping, which meant that we would see a lot less conflict than previous deployments. We had been informed of that shift ahead of time, but I still expected to encounter some sort of conflict or excitement. However, during the entire time I was in Afghanistan, I never personally shot my rifle. We did encounter indirect fire (IDF, as we call it), which came close, and I know it mentally affected some of our men. Our guard towers were shot at fairly frequently, but that was about it where conflict was concerned.

Our unit was assigned to different weekly shifts, which included tasks like guard duty. That mostly involved a rotating watch between the four guard towers. When we weren't in one of the towers, we were expected to work the camp's entrance, where we'd pat down or x-ray visitors, check cars entering the base, and patrol the area. Guard duty wasn't bad at all, unless the weather was against us. The winter was freezing since there were no heaters in the towers. We'd spend our time shivering and trying to stay warm by doing push-ups or wrestling.

After a week of guard duty, we usually transitioned to a shift on the Quick Response Force (QRF), an armed unit expected to be ready to respond to any developing situation or emergency.

If it was QRF week, we would be on call and ready for anything that might happen. We'd stay in a small tent and keep our armour on all the time, waiting for a call to go out and assist. We did a lot of training during this time too, preparing for situations where we'd need to get people down from towers quickly or out of bunk rooms and into cars.

The third week in the rotation was for Force Protection Element work. Those weeks, we would jump into our PMVs (personal mobility vehicles) with officers and drive about two or three kilometres to the camp where Afghan National Army members were training to become officers. Our officers would go in and teach while my crew commander and I would position ourselves just outside and let the infantry team roam around, making sure that nothing bad could happen to the people inside, and securing the area as much as we could.

If there was any downtime during these three-week rotations, we would do things like organise a convoy to go to Camp KAIA to pick up mail. We perfected the art of getting to Camp KAIA unbelievably fast, less than twenty minutes compared to others' forty-minute trips. Sometimes we'd stay at Camp KAIA for a bit, playing volleyball or soccer (we had a gym and Ping-Pong table at our camp, but nothing like their setup) or going out to dinner there. Then we'd head back as fast as we arrived. It was always nice when we could get a break from the food at Camp KARGA, which was greasy and not good at all. At the end of our seven-month deployment, I think we were all so happy to be able to eat vegetables again. Everything we'd been served was mass-made and not particularly healthy.

One of my best memories was when it first snowed during our deployment. Many of the Australians had never seen snow before, so when it happened, we all ran outside and stared into the sky. As the snow accumulated, we had a massive snowball fight for a good thirty to forty-five minutes. We took the lids off of metal rubbish bins and turned them into shields; we used shovels as catapults. Other people started picking up anything they could to join in the fight; some of the guys even put on helmets or parts of their body armour. Along the way, our snowball fight became half children's game, half brutal conflict. We were all having so much fun—and glad for the release.

A few of the Americans and the UK guys looked on, asking, "What the hell is going on?"

In our defence, one of our officers said, "They've never seen snow. What are you expecting?"

Most of our deployment, we just tried to fill the minutes and hours. Although we arrived thinking we'd all be super busy, the fact was that there wasn't a lot to do. Being on guard in the towers, especially, left us with considerable downtime. It was during my time up there that I had the bandwidth and space to start confronting my own mental health.

Beginning in my teens, I had gotten into the habit of having a yearly mental breakdown. I'd become overwhelmed thinking about my childhood, my mother, and my lack of any real father. I'd lie in bed, crying the entire night while thinking about my bullies and the way my body was growing and changing.

I wanted to figure out why I was so unloved and unworthy—why I felt like an inconvenience to everybody around me. I wanted to know what I could do better and why I hated myself so much. During those episodes, the noises that came out of my throat didn't even sound like me. It was such an angry, all-consuming cry, and so much heat would emanate that even my hands would become covered in sweat.

As the breakdowns continued, they began to take a particular shape. I'd often think of a topic, and dig deep, asking myself *why* over and over: *Why is this happening to me? Why do I cry?* These yearly breakdowns would also sometimes include suicidal thoughts. In hindsight, I don't think I ever really wanted to kill myself; it was more that I just wanted to disappear. What somehow made it worse was the thought that no one would care if I ever did. But at least these thoughts never progressed to me actually harming myself.

As quickly as these annual breakdowns began, they would also end. Eventually, I'd fall asleep, and the next morning I'd wake up feeling fine. Then, I'd spend the next 364 days feeling mostly okay. But underneath the surface, my depression and anxiety were slowly building, and eventually the breakdown would happen all over again. At the time, I thought these emotional episodes were helpful—that it was good I was getting out all of my feelings. It never occurred to me to seek professional help or support in any way. Despite asking myself tough questions once a year, I was still burying my feelings most of the time.

Once I arrived in Afghanistan, I began to really think about my mental health. When we were on tower lookout, I got into the habit of recording myself on my GoPro, talking about what I was experiencing on deployment or things I'd gone through in the past. These sessions with myself seemed to be the start of something productive. All it took was for me to be a little bored up in those towers to decide it was a good time to finally get started with my personal inventory. One of the things that motivated me to start doing this work was my relationship with a crew commander. Even though he outranked me (he was a corporal), he tended to mess up a lot, and I would end up having to take the blame. That created a real lack of trust, along with some resentment on my part. In one particular instance, the corporal led our convoy down the wrong road, and our vehicles became stuck—something that was normally very unlikely to happen. We had to get a chain and pull ourselves out that day. Other times, he would have no idea where he was leading us. In a war zone, you have to be aware of your surroundings, especially in a lead vehicle. His lack of awareness made the rest of us feel unsafe.

The corporal also tended to overreact. In Middle Eastern countries like Afghanistan, residents will sometimes hold big weddings with thousands of guests celebrating over the course of several days. When Afghanis see wedding-decorated cars driving by, they'll whistle a horn or make noise to signal, *We're celebrating!* But my crew commander didn't realise this, and when wedding guests were near our vehicle, he would overreact, potentially placing everyone in danger. In training, we'd been taught that whenever people got too close to a convoy, our first action should be to use our hands to signal for them to stop, then motion for the people to back off. If that didn't work, we were supposed to use the laser on our assault rifle to indicate, *Hey, we mean it. Don't come any closer.* If that still didn't work, we had water bottles we could throw to get the people to back off. If none of those tactics worked, we would use a pen flare. The last and most drastic step would be to shoot. Our training instructions were very specific about this order of increasing aggression and how it should be used. However, at this particular wedding, my crew commander authorised the use of the pen flare right away.

"What on earth are you doing?" I called out. "It's a fucking wedding, man!"

Everyone heard, and it seemed like I was undermining his authority, an offence that could come with a heavy consequence in the military. But I didn't care; situations like that drove me mad—and could have gotten us killed.

In the most disturbing situation with this corporal, we had just finished a convoy. He was on top of our vehicle, where a .50-caliber machine gun was mounted. After each mission, we were supposed to take down the gun, stow it inside the vehicle, then lock up the vehicle to make sure everything was secure. Instead, the corporal hopped off without the gun. We locked the vehicle, and I had the key because I was the driver. I had no idea the gun was still on top.

This was a QRF week, and when we got a call about a helicopter landing, we went back to the truck, got in, and I realised the gun, which we called "the fifty," wasn't there anymore.

"What happened? Where is the fifty?" I asked the corporal.

"I have no idea," he said. "I must have left it up top."

"Well, where did it go?!" Now *I* was the one screaming. "We can't just tell a helicopter to turn around. We need to go!"

I immediately ran to where the other corporals were posted.

"Do you guys have the fifty in here?" I asked.

"It's here," one of them said. "Was it you that left it?"

"We don't have time to go through this right now," I responded. "Let's discuss it when I come back."

"No," said one of the corporals. "It's your crew commander's responsibility. He has to come get it."

In the interest of saving time, I said, "You know what? It

was my fault. He asked me to lock it up, and I'm the one who screwed up. I'll face the consequences when I get back."

The corporal handed me the gun, I got back to the truck, and we drove down to the helicopter landing. I ended up getting a warning for that one. The crew commander thanked me and told me he appreciated my taking the blame. Turned out, he already had a warning or two under his belt. But even with his show of gratitude, our relationship had become more strained. I hadn't had a discipline problem prior to that. However, as fate would have it, I'd have two more issues arise in the next few days. In one instance, I was on guard duty. My shift usually ended around 5:00 or 6:00 p.m., and on this particular occasion, I didn't take my night vision goggles since I knew I wouldn't need them. For some reason, an infantry guy I was with complained to our sergeant that my decision made me a liability, particularly if we had to unexpectedly stay there overnight. The sergeant agreed, and I was reprimanded. Then a few days later, I overslept for a guard shift. All three events compounded and got me charged with soldier negligence. Basically, the charge said I wasn't living up to the standards of what a soldier is. I took it as a sign they were trying to get rid of me, and I became determined not to get in any more trouble for anything, no matter what. I was going to be on top of absolutely everything.

It wasn't long after this formal charge and my terrible week of mishaps and getting into trouble that I started with the GoPro videos. On those recordings, I kept asking myself, "Why does this get me angry?" and "Why does this make me sad?" I'd let myself go down the rabbit hole of emotions, all the way to the thoughts of not being worthy. There I was, standing in my military uniform in a tower in Afghanistan and taking myself all the way back to that scene where my mum was screaming about my attempts to take my mattress after she'd kicked me out. Standing in the tower and recording myself with my GoPro, I'd let myself fully feel those emotions of not being worthy and of having a mother who hated me. Then, a few days later, I'd replay those tapes and realise how hard I was being on myself. In time, I began to understand that my self-criticism wasn't fair. Instead, I started using the tapes to help me pinpoint whatever it was that was triggering me to think and talk that way. I was on a mission to hunt down why my mind was going in those directions. Once I had any insight, I'd write it down and see what I could learn from it.

These recordings were freeing, scary, and sometimes even funny when I listened to my own words repeated back to me. I don't think I realised until that moment what a screwup I thought myself to be. I'd spent so much of my life wanting to become someone who was proud, strong, brave, and lovable. Yet here I was talking about all my mistakes and how I wasn't even worthy to be deployed in the military because I couldn't be part of a team and play along. It was real self-therapy, and it was one of the greatest things I took from my seven months in Afghanistan.

By the time of my deployment, it had been several years since I'd last heard from my mother. One day, out of the blue, I received a letter from her. Up to that point, I'd grown accustomed to never receiving letters or care packages. When that envelope was handed to me, I was shocked. To this day, I still don't know how she knew where I was or how she got my mailing address. Opening that envelope, I hoped it might contain an apology or at least a note saying how proud my mum was to know that I was serving in the military. I guess I shouldn't have been surprised that it said neither, but it still hurt. Towards the end of the letter, she asked me two questions. When I looked again at the envelope, I realised it had no return address on it;

even if I'd wanted to respond, there was no way I could. The letter did help spark a few new GoPro self-examination videos, so at least I could count it as more progress on my mental health journey. However, as I would later come to find out, I'd have to really hit rock bottom before I could ever make any real progress on that front.

CHAPTER 4

AS OUR DEPLOYMENT IN AFGHANISTAN CAME TO AN END, I had to confront an unexpected sensation: instead of feeling proud, I mostly felt unfulfilled. I'd been dissatisfied at so many other points in my life, but I'd also always assumed the military would be different. I didn't know how to rid myself of that feeling, but I knew I needed to find a way—and quickly.

Our unit returned to Australia on a military plane. After we landed at the tiny Townsville airport, we were all brought into a room for a debriefing. There, our superiors told us what to expect when we walked through the doors into the main terminal of the airport; namely, that we would see a lot of emotional friends and family members, along with enthusiastic fanfare over our arrival. I barely listened to this description. I knew it was unlikely anyone had come out to meet me personally, and mostly I was just excited to be back in my home country. Once the doors to the concourse opened, it was as if a plane filled with celebrities had just arrived: all you could see were camera flashes and TV crews. Families lined up behind them, many holding signs with their soldiers' names on them or waving banners in the air. People were clapping and crying and hugging, which made the emptiness of my return that much more apparent. I'd never expected that anyone would be there for me, but I'd also hoped that my friends would prove me wrong.

As I grabbed my luggage, I briefly regarded the people waiting for their loved ones and then ducked away from the crowd. It just felt easier to board the awaiting coach and drown out the scene with some music piped through my headphones. While I waited for the coach to depart, I hopped on Facebook Messenger to see if I could connect with any military friends who might be in Townsville. Turns out, a bunch of them were out partying—and not too far from the airport. Learning that news stung. They knew I was returning, and I was disappointed they hadn't made the effort to drive the short distance to greet me. Instead, they invited me to join them for a night on the town, but I didn't feel up to it. I just wanted to go back and get some sleep, unpack my suitcase, and get out of a military mindset for a few hours.

I'd left the keys to my place with Tobi while I'd been deployed so that if friends were coming to visit from out of town, they could use my room instead of having to get their own accommodations. Now when I opened the door to my room, it became immediately clear that people had been staying without cleaning up after themselves. All my things were out of order, and the room looked trashed. That alone was a further excuse for me not to join up with Tobi and our other friends that night. I was angry no one had taken care of my room while I was gone.

Looking back on that day, I wonder now if I'm partly to blame for the lack of reception I received at the airport. The people closest to me knew I'd be returning that day, but I hadn't specifically asked them to come. Part of me just assumed they would want to be there—that they should have shown up automatically. I knew when it came to the people I cared about that I would always make the effort to show up. They were my priority, and I wanted them to know that. Knowing that my friends were out having a typical night of fun made it seem like partying was more important than greeting me at the airport. I had become used to doing many things on my own and without much recognition—flying to visit friends, only to have no one there to greet me at the airport; paying twenty dollars to park my car and pick up a friend who was visiting, only to have them head off and do their own thing. But I still thought it would be nice if people could really show up for me. I'd sometimes think how it wasn't hard to look after someone, help them out, and be there for them, but for some reason when it came to me, people often made it feel like it was just too much bother.

In the end, I decided the only way I could have a truly spectacular welcome-home party was if I threw one for myself. I knew if I was going to go big, I needed to make it as over the top as I possibly could. So I rented a penthouse at one of the best hotels on Australia's Gold Coast and leased a yacht for a private party. I made dinner reservations at expensive restaurants, planned cocktails at exclusive bars, and hired strippers for after-hours entertainment. And then I invited all of my closest mates. Most of them said, "There's no way I can afford any of that." But I'd saved up all my combat pay and wanted to spend it on the people I cared about. The total bill came to at least $10,000, and I told my mates to pay whatever they could. For some of them, that was only about $150, but it didn't matter—I was just glad to be having a good time and creating a spectacular weekend for everyone else. A few of the guys I'd served alongside in Afghanistan came as well; later, they told me it was one of the best weekends of their lives. That meant a lot to me.

After the high of this lavish weekend, the emotional impact of my deployment and subsequent return began to sink in. My life in the military felt mundane—boring even. The army had just received a new fleet of Mercedes G-Wagons and armoured trucks to replace our aging Land Rovers. Everyone who might have to use the new vehicles had to be trained on them first, and my job was to teach those classes. Most of my students were senior officers—people with a lot more rank than I would ever have. When teaching them, I was supposed to follow a prewritten script, but it was ridiculous and clearly written for new recruits, not for seasoned officers who had been driving cars longer than I'd been alive. I knew there was absolutely no need to teach them the proper way to parallel park or to execute a three-point turn, nor was I going to bore them with information about the width of the car or how much it weighed. Instead, I devised my own curriculum.

"Look," I'd say on the first day of class. "I'm going to teach you the safety aspects of this vehicle and what it's really capable of so that you never have to worry when you're out in the field."

My first course evaluations were incredibly positive. The officers loved it.

My second course was with officers with even higher ranks than those in my first section. They loved it, too, and wrote more enthusiastic evaluations. Some of the evals made it all the way to the army's head of transport, who contacted my supervisor. My boss wanted to know what I was doing to make all those officers so happy, so he came down to watch one of my lessons. During one of the breaks, I could tell he wasn't impressed.

"You can't do that," he scolded. "You have to follow the rules."

"Fair enough," I replied. What else could I have said?

I knew some of the participants had probably heard our conversation, so after the break, I went back and told them I had to redo the lesson—and this time totally by the assigned script.

"I'll be teaching as per the ADI book," I told them, referencing a dense and mostly useless manual on driving.

Then I proceeded to read from the prepared script. It couldn't have been more boring. And the officers knew it. One of them took my supervisor aside and gave him a good lecture, making it clear that he thought my approach to the course was much better and that my boss had been unfairly censoring me. Not long after, the head of transportation came to congratulate me and offer me a position in her office, but by then, it didn't matter. My boss felt like I had embarrassed him and failed to observe the chain of command. From then on, he began to look for increasingly menial jobs to fill my days. After he ordered me to sweep leaves during a cyclone (a truly impossible and ridiculous task), I knew I'd had enough. I felt completely unproductive. The only other way I could feel fulfilled in the military was to get deployed into an actual war zone where I would have the opportunity to defend against a firefight. However, by then, it was 2015, and the face of war in the Middle East had changed. Firefights were largely a thing of the past.

And so, when my posting was finished in Townsville, I decided to resign from the military. I knew it wasn't serving me well anymore, and I wanted to challenge myself. Leaving the army ended up being much easier than I had thought it might be. My original contract was for twelve months, and I had already served nearly four years. So I was soon discharged and set to leave Townsville. I left knowing that I needed a change: something bigger and more meaningful. Something that could fill my soul. One thing kept coming to my mind: travel. I decided to follow that instinct and head to Africa, where

I could have a real adventure gorilla trekking or exploring the jungle. One night, not long before I departed, I met up with some friends to say goodbye. While we were out, my friend Pete told me I was crazy; he thought that my plan was ridiculous and needlessly dangerous. I told him that I'd at least make the news if I died trekking.

"If I were given the chance to read one of two articles, one with the headline 'Australian killed in Afghanistan' and the other reading 'Australian tourist ripped apart by wild gorilla,' I know which of the two articles I'd read," I told Pete.

A few of our friends laughed, but I was being half-serious. The military had turned out to be mostly a joke for me; travelling would at least be real. Just before my deployment, Tobi, Amber, and I had taken a holiday to Machu Picchu. The day before our tour was set to start, the three of us were hanging out in Buenos Aires. We knew that robberies were common there, but we'd also heard that they were rarely armed crimes. Besides, the three of us were soldiers; we thought we knew how to protect ourselves. Nevertheless, that day while we were walking back to our hotel, two guys on a motorbike approached us. One of them brandished a pistol and demanded our valuables. My adrenaline immediately kicked in, and my only reaction was to fight back. I started fistfighting with one of them, refusing to give him anything, including my bag. He demanded my camera. I'd still wanted to refuse, but something told me it might be better just to hand it over. As I went to surrender it, the strap got caught on my hand. *Perfect*, I thought. *Now I'm just going to smash the camera. If I can't have it, neither can they.* I threw it on the ground, and it shattered.

The next thing I knew, Amber was screaming. The other man, the guy who had a pistol, was hounding her and wasn't afraid to harass us with it. He was trying to take Amber's sunnies and wallet. This sent my adrenaline even higher. As I approached him, he pointed the pistol directly at me. He hit me in the back of the neck with it, but I hardly felt it. He hit me again and then pointed the gun right at my face. I stood my ground. Eventually, he backed up, got on his motorcycle, and rode off with only Amber's sunnies in hand. The other guy took off too, and I chased them in my flip-flops, throwing rocks at them and shouting at passersby for not doing anything to help us. Later, Tobi, Amber, and I laughed about how I'd refused to hand over my bag. At the time, I'd thought it contained my passport. Only later did I remember it was filled entirely with dirty clothes. But even if I'd remembered that during the actual robbery, I don't know that it would have changed anything; there was no way I was going to let those guys take anything from me—or from my friends. Given a choice, I would have taken a bullet simply to defend us and our things—even if those things were just a pair of sunnies and a smelly bag of laundry.

Afterwards, we went to the police station to file a report. While we were waiting for an officer, Amber asked if I was okay.

"Yeah, I'm fine." I said. "Why?"

"Your hands are bleeding," she explained. It was only then that I realised how intense that fistfight had been.

The officers who interviewed us assumed this had been a typical robbery where locals trick a tourist and take something of theirs while they're distracted. When I explained that these assailants had a gun, I could see their disbelief.

"Why did you fight back?" one of them asked.

I explained that we'd just finished our deployment training and were soldiers who'd been taught to protect ourselves.

That trip to Argentina had been the kind of adrenaline-filled experience and sense of accomplishment I'd been hoping for in Afghanistan. Once I returned home, I knew the best chance of re-creating that sensation would be to travel again. I was willing to spend whatever on flights, accommodations, and tours. I wanted to be back out in the world, seeing and doing everything I'd ever dreamed about. So, I decided to become a nomad ticking off a bucket list and enjoying the kinds of experiences very few people ever had. I even took myself off the electoral roll in Australia, figuring it could be a long time before I returned.

By then, I had just a backpack and a single suitcase of belongings and no real place to call home. It was liberating: I could go wherever, whenever. I already had a few places at the top of my list, including Central Africa, Canada, Egypt, Scandinavia, and Russia. Mostly, I travelled alone. But I rarely felt lonely. It was almost always easy to find people to chat with and to make friends on my travels. I also spared no expense on these trips. While I was in St. Petersburg, for instance, my tour manager easily persuaded me to splurge on tickets for the Russian ballet.

"You probably won't be back anytime soon, so why not spend the money while you're here?" he reasoned. "Even if you don't like it, you'll go home richer in experience."

I took that advice to heart and told myself it was how I should always live my life.

On the trip to Africa after my military discharge, adventure always seemed to have a way of finding me. I spent some of the holiday on a fifty-eight-day tour of Kenya, Uganda, and then all the way south to Cape Town. The tour was on the back of an Overlander truck, and we camped each night somewhere along the route. When we were in Uganda, the roads we travelled on were narrow and not well maintained. One day, while we were riding along the side of a steep cliff, our truck hit a bump, causing the back end to fishtail dangerously. When we finally came to a stop, the back of the truck was nearly hanging over the edge of the cliff. I was sitting in the very back of the truck, and as I craned my neck to look down into the abyss, all I could think was, *I'm going to be the first of us to die.* Quickly, my childhood desire to be a hero took over. I wanted everyone safe, so I immediately told everyone to get off the truck.

"I don't have my shoes," someone on the tour said, as she blocked the aisle for others to get out.

"We can't worry about your shoes!" I responded in disbelief. I couldn't fathom someone would jeopardise the safety of others over something as insignificant as a pair of shoes.

The truck didn't end up falling, and everyone was fine, but it was definitely too close for comfort. We ended up needing a machine to come pull the truck out safely while we waited on the side of the cliff, talking and eventually laughing about what a close call it had been.

The next day we went gorilla trekking. The hike to see the gorillas was through dense jungle. For part of it, we managed to follow a cleared elephant trail, but soon we had to use other shortcuts, including walking or sliding down the side of mountains and back up the other side. Much of the journey seemed like a Hollywood pirate movie, with those leading our pack using machetes to cut through the jungle.

It took about five hours of this before we finally reached the gorillas.

@THECONVOYER

QR code for Instagram videos and colourised graphics.

The gorilla family we found had only been introduced to humans about a week or two earlier. Although the leaders of our trip had machetes for clearing the jungle, the rest of us were told we couldn't carry sticks or anything that could look like a weapon or might seem aggressive to the gorillas. When it came time to approach them, we watched as they gradually became comfortable with us. They started coming out slowly from behind branches so thick you'd need an axe to chop them down. Soon, about thirty gorillas had assembled right around us. As the adults munched on leaves, a baby gorilla came right up to us. When the baby was just seconds from touching our feet, his father—a silverback—came rushing past and picked him up. Most of us felt the tension and backed away.

However, one of the guys on our trip thought this would be a great opportunity for a photograph, so he started approaching the gorillas with his camera. First, the silverback started grunting at him, and then another gorilla charged him. The gorilla was going crazy, picking up giant branches as thick as my legs and throwing them in the air. We all slowly backed up further. I'll never forget the experience of having that gorilla look me dead in the eye. I knew it wouldn't take much for him to kill me. My heart definitely stopped for a minute; it was all unreal but also a meaningful experience I'll always keep with me.

The adrenaline didn't stop flowing there. While in Dar es Salaam, Tanzania, I asked around about the best place to get a haircut and a shave. Eventually, someone directed me to a seedy barbershop. As the barber finished my shave, he put what I thought was aftershave on my cheeks and chin. But as soon as it was applied, I began to feel faint. I was sure I was going to pass out, and all I kept thinking to myself was, *Okay, focus, pay, and get the hell out of here!* I somehow made it outside and to the side of the building where no one could see me. It took all of my concentration and energy to walk as straight as possible and not fall over. Once I was out of view, I gripped the building with both hands. I was terrified they'd given me something or put some kind of drug in the aftershave. I worried I was going to pass out, and I knew from previous fainting experiences that that was a distinct possibility. Who knew what would happen to me if I did? Thankfully, I made it back to camp safely. Later, we all had a laugh about it, but in that moment, I was certain I saw my life at a crossroads where it could be changed forever.

Sunset in Zanzibar.

Sandboarding in Namibia.

Three months later, I made it to Egypt. I went to one of the temples in Alexandria, and I nearly got lost in one of the tombs. There were no guards inside, and hardly any other tourists around since many would-be visitors had been discouraged by the possibility of a terrorist attack. Alone and feeling lost, I wandered that tomb for what felt like hours, trying to find my way out. I was knee-deep in water before I turned around.

Then, I nearly got attacked by stray dogs before I found an exit. Once I was outside, I was able to put more distance between the strays and myself, but then they began encircling me. I picked up rocks to throw in their direction, hoping that would make them leave me alone, but it didn't work. It wasn't until I reached the front gate, about two hundred metres from where I'd exited, that one of the guards there started waving his security baton at the dogs to scare them off. By then, I knew I was safe. In hindsight, I felt proud I'd kept my cool and figured out a solution on my own.

Pyramids of Giza.

All of this travel also made me realise I didn't need a family to be able to do whatever I wanted to do. Instead, I was making it happen for myself. I began living for the thrill of it all. I loved experiencing new countries and airports, along with different languages, foods, and natural adventures. During these trips,

I managed to distract my mind from the emotional pain I'd been experiencing for so long. But of course, the things that plague you don't just completely go away. One night in Malawi, my tour group and I stopped at Kande Beach, located on Lake Malawi, a giant, crystal-clear lake. It's a spectacular place with great campsites and restaurants, so a lot of tour groups tend to meet up there. On that particular night, we'd all had quite a bit to drink. I became overwhelmed by all the emotions I'd been bottling up, and when the group went to sleep, I had a sudden urge to write a poem.

> *Sitting here in the night of a thousand stars,*
> *Never-ending eyes and never-ending light,*
> *The game and wild run free,*
> *Yet the privee and the stolen run captive.*
> *How do we extinguish the hungry and the lonely?*
> *Only by secluding the lonely and heartless,*
> *Do we find a kindness given by the hungry,*
> *And send free the lonely.*

I wasn't really sure what I was trying to say, but I know I must have dug far into my soul for it—even in my drunken stupor. About three weeks later, I shared it with a few people in our group. "That's really deep," one of them said. I was pleasantly surprised that, even in my drunken state, I had written something that resonated with someone.

On this tour, a fellow traveller happened to be employed as a trip manager for Contiki, the travel company that took eighteen-to-thirty-five-year-olds on group tours around the world. She tried to persuade me to apply for a position with them.

"You'd love it," she told me. "You'll get paid to travel."

I kept her offer in the back of my mind, thinking it could be an option once my money ran out, especially since I now had a contact there. But in the meantime, I knew I had more of the world to see—and on my own terms.

It took a couple more months before I was ready to consider settling down for a while. My sister Lea was living back in France, not far from the border with Switzerland, so I decided to move in with her for a bit and began applying for a variety of jobs: everything from bartending in Switzerland to housesitting in Iceland.

While I waited to hear back, I got a job at an English-speaking bar in Lausanne, probably forty minutes away from Lea's place. The owner told me I'd be paid under the table and would be making something like twenty-five francs an hour (which is about thirty-four dollars Australian). For someone with my lifestyle, that was a lot of money. I found my own apartment on Lake Geneva and was certain I finally had it made. But rent was difficult to pay, since I'd spent nearly all of my savings on travel, and the owner of the bar kept refusing to pay me. I kept trying to explain this to my landlady, but she understandably wanted her money.

Soon, I was broke. It became clear that my time in the Lake Geneva apartment, as well as my time at that bar, would be very short-lived. That was when I remembered the traveller on the African Safari tour who had recommended working at Contiki, so I decided to apply there. Within twelve hours, I got the job and booked a plane ticket to Lyon to start work at the Contiki Chateau there. But first, I had to ask my friend Denise back in Australia for a loan to pay off my Swiss landlady. I swore to Denise I'd pay her back after I received my first Contiki paycheck.

Although I was excited about the new job, I also had some

doubts. Contiki is a hugely successful company, but they're also known for catering to a heavy-drinking clientele. More often than not, customers leave their excursions with a severe hangover and next to no memory of how they spent their two-, three-, or even five-week trip. In the end, I decided it was still worth it. The Contiki Chateau was in the valley of the Beaujolais French wine region, and my job there was easy. All the drinks were two dollars, and when I wasn't handing out drinks, I was housekeeping, doing the dishes, and sometimes cooking meals. I liked the work and the opportunity to chat with guests. Being fluent in French also made it easy to talk with locals and deal with any deliveries or the occasional hospital visit, due to the travellers injuring themselves on their drunken nights out.

There were some bleak times, however. One winter, I agreed to serve as a desk clerk at a Contiki hub in London known as "The Basement." Beginning at about five o'clock each morning, I would welcome guests, show them to their rooms, and give them the Wi-Fi information and directions to the bathroom. The job didn't require you to be a rocket scientist, and the pay reflected that. Given how expensive it was to live in London, on my salary there was no way I was going to be able to rent a flat. Some of my coworkers stayed in hotel rooms, but I couldn't find one in my price range. It didn't take long before I was down to my last few hundred pounds. The way I saw it, I had two obvious choices: I could go back and live with Lea, or I could spend the last of my money on a one-way ticket back to Australia and start all over again. Neither option appealed to me. I decided to suck it up and stay in London, no matter what it took. After my shifts ended each afternoon, I'd walk around the city, trying to stay warm. At night, after the other employees left, I'd grab a discarded sleeping bag some guest had left and sleep on the floor of our staff locker room—a room accessible by code and where our on-road crews could store their personal belongings. It wasn't comfortable, but at least I knew I wouldn't freeze to death. I knew I risked losing my job by sleeping in there; at any time someone could enter the room and stumble upon me trying to get some sleep. Only once, though, did someone come in; luckily, they didn't notice me. At that point, though, I knew I needed a better arrangement.

I decided to apply for Contiki's on-road crew. If I got the job, I would become a tour driver around Europe. I would be getting paid to travel, along with tips and free accommodations. I figured it couldn't possibly be any harder than driving a military vehicle. Plus, I wouldn't have to pay for meals or drinks, so the position seemed perfect. That spring, I learned that I'd been hired for the position and needed to report for on-road training.

Between my military experience, my background travelling throughout Europe, and my ability to speak multiple languages, I felt confident that I'd be a great Contiki driver. I began to study for my coach license while bouncing around in other roles for the company. Aside from parallel parking, driving the coach was no problem, but the other training was intense. You had to know about the places you were visiting and how to get not only from point A to point B, but also points C through Z as well. Using Google Maps wasn't an option, so you also had to memorise every exit, all the turns, and which roads were big enough to accommodate our huge coaches.

As a new driver, I did three long trips for Contiki: one was forty-five days, one was thirty-seven days, and another was twenty-five days. The trips went all over, starting from London and then moving on to Barcelona, France, Italy, Greece, Istanbul, Serbia, Dubrovnik, the Netherlands—you name it. By then, I was twenty-three and still always happy to be on the move. I loved discovering the history of every place we visited, and I learned a lot from our trip managers, who taught me and the guests about each area. It felt great to be constantly learning something new.

My new job also came with some hilarious mishaps—especially early on. On one trip, another coach and I were trying to pull out at the same time, and the side mirror of his coach crashed through one of my windows. On another, I didn't see a bollard next to where my coach was parked, and I smashed my door into it when I tried to open it. The door wouldn't work properly after that, so I cut the wires in an attempt to override the automatic system. Apparently, I didn't know quite as much about electrical work as I thought, because I didn't isolate the correct wires, and the coach wouldn't turn back on. We were stranded until Contiki could send us another coach. But that kind of thing happened so frequently that Contiki always had a quick backup plan, and there were never any bad consequences for me.

Some of my previous life experiences definitely came in handy in situations like those. I'd learned to be good at problem-solving, and I knew how to stay calm in difficult situations. If I needed to organise taxis for everyone, I could. I could clean up a messy situation and get the paperwork done whenever necessary. I also loved having sustained time with guests. My first trip was a camping expedition throughout Europe: from London to Barcelona to Istanbul to Serbia and the Netherlands. At each destination, I'd pull out all the tents and help get everything set up. This set of clients was a high-energy group, and we really bonded during that time. Whenever anyone asked, I'd tell them I'd been driving coaches for years and never let on that this was my first time. At the end of that initial tour, the leader conducted a debrief and asked if anyone wanted to admit to telling a lie on the trip. I stepped forward.

"Okay, guys," I began. "I've been telling you that I've been driving coaches for five or six years. But the truth is, I got my license a couple of months ago, and you're my first trip."

The participants were dumbfounded. "No fucking way," a few of them said. "You've got to be kidding me."

I took that as a compliment; I figured they couldn't believe I was brand new. When the trip manager told them he was new as well, they were ecstatic. But I had to wonder: how did it feel to find out you'd put your life in the hands of a young guy who'd never before driven a coach filled with passengers around Europe?

Halfway through my second long trip, things started to feel repetitive. It got exhausting to constantly be around a big group of drunk people, essentially when it felt like I was just babysitting them. But then things got crazy. It was the summer of 2017, and I was driving a group through Barcelona, where I was conducting a city tour. Barcelona is a beautiful place filled with history and stunning architecture. The clients and I were all enjoying the scenery and listening to the trip manager, who was telling us about the city, when I began to notice that the cars around us were driving erratically and moving too fast for conditions. Some of the defensive driving techniques I learned in Afghanistan rushed back into my head; something was clearly wrong, and although I couldn't figure out exactly what was happening, I knew it had the potential to escalate quickly. I slowed the coach and began to survey the scene. As we approached the centre of the city, I saw what looked like SWAT cars lining a street. This was clearly serious.

"I think I'm going to turn around," I said to my trip manager. "Something's not right."

"I agree," he said, clearly concerned. Within a minute of us turning around, his phone started ringing. We both looked at each other, wide-eyed.

He answered, spoke quickly, and then hung up. "We need to get back to the hotel," he said. "Now!"

It was then that we learned someone had driven a van into a crowd of people, killing fifteen and injuring 130. I knew my first priority was our clients. I pulled the coach up to our hotel so that my passengers could disembark, and then I went to park the coach a few blocks away, where it would hopefully be safe overnight. From there, I started heading back on foot to the hotel. Somehow, I ended up walking directly back to where the attack had happened. Soon, I was overwhelmed by the sound of sirens and the cries of injured people. Medical professionals raced around, trying to tend to survivors. The scene was almost like a battlefield, the ground covered in bodies along with a lot of blood and debris.

@THECONVOYER

QR code for Instagram videos and colourised graphics.

Something in my brain went right back to my childhood goal of helping people. That impulse had only grown stronger since Afghanistan and my time in Africa, and I saw in this opportunity a real chance to help—to be the hero I'd always believed I could be. However, because I didn't speak Spanish, I couldn't figure out what anyone needed. People raced up to me, speaking urgently, but I couldn't make out what they were saying. Instead, all I could do was tell them I didn't understand.

"Do you speak English?" I'd ask hopefully. Frustrated, they'd quickly move on to someone who could understand their words. By then, the street was crawling with police and first responders, so I decided the best thing I could do was return to the hotel and be with our Contiki group.

I managed to hail a taxi, which I shared with someone from the scene. We couldn't really communicate, but I could tell by the way they were acting that they were pretty shaken up. Once I made it back to the hotel, the trip manager and I got everyone rounded up and led them to the rooftop of the hotel. Along the way, we grabbed four jugs of beer to help calm everyone's nerves. Up on the rooftop, we told them to have a drink while we explained what had happened.

"You can each make your decision individually about whether you'd like to stay on the tour or if you want to go home," we told them. "If you want to call your parents, you can do that, too, and if you don't have a phone, you can use ours."

"Are we safe?" one of the travellers asked. "What do you recommend?"

"I believe we are as safe as can be," I told them honestly. "Attacks like these are often like lightning; they don't strike the same place twice."

At the time, we weren't sure if the attack on the crowded street was actually a terrorist attack or perhaps just a crazy driver, but we knew it wasn't good either way. We were able to keep everyone's emotions under control, though, and it bonded us as a group. I think only one or two of the group decided to go home—everybody else stayed and enjoyed the rest of our trip. Their decision to put their trust in us gave me a lot of confidence; it was proof I could keep my cool in a crisis, take care of my people, and make decisions that would keep us all happy and safe.

CHAPTER 5

BY THE END OF MY THIRD CONTIKI TRIP, I'D HAD ENOUGH. Driving drunk travellers around Europe was getting old. Some of them didn't even remember our trips to the big attractions, like the Eiffel Tower and the Colosseum. The way I saw it, if these travellers couldn't even bother to remember a trip, they might as well have stayed home and drank with friends. Europe is there to be explored, not forgotten over a drunken holiday.

I called my friend Tobi. "I'm having another one of those existential crises," I told him. "I don't know what I want to do, but I do know that I don't want to do this job anymore. I feel stuck."

"Listen, you're doing exactly what you said you wanted to do when you left Townsville," Tobi reminded me. "You said, 'I'm going to travel the world, and I'm going to get a job that pays me to do it.' That's exactly what you're doing."

I knew he was right, but I still couldn't stop my mind from feeling restless. I wanted more. I *needed* more. I just wasn't yet sure what, exactly, I was looking for.

Not long after that phone call, I returned to Switzerland. There, I met my childhood friend Clara, along with her parents, Miguel and Sandrine, for dinner. Over the course of the meal, I told them how dissatisfied I had begun feeling about my job.

"I need a change," I said. "I want adventure, and driving drunk tourists around isn't working for me. Maybe I'll go back to the army, or maybe try the federal police."

"I have an idea for you," Miguel said. "What about a humanitarian organisation?"

The suggestion confused me. I'd always assumed humanitarian organisations were about healthcare. "Wouldn't I have to have some trained medical experience or something?"

Miguel explained that this particular humanitarian organisation is a private, neutral humanitarian aid organisation responsible for all kinds of work around the world.

"They do everything," Miguel said. "Logistics. Warehousing. Healthcare. Education. They have mechanics, too. I'm sure they're always looking for people."

I had always viewed Miguel as a kind of father figure. He had three daughters, and I think he might have wanted to mentor a boy as well. When I think back on my childhood, he was one of the most influential male figures I'd had while living in Switzerland. So when he suggested the organisation, I definitely listened. I began reading about the organisation and learned that they do aid work primarily in third-world countries. Because of their status as the world's leading and largest humanitarian organisation, they can often get permission to enter areas impacted by war or natural disasters that many state or other private groups can't. I was impressed by their size and the sheer scope of their work: the organisation works privately and is often one of the first groups on the ground in compromised and war-torn countries.

I also noticed there was an open position for a vehicle fleet manager, a role that was likely above my knowledge base, but I figured my experience in the military and my job driving coaches for Contiki could both get my application noticed. To be honest, I never thought I'd be seriously considered for the job, especially after I learned how well respected they are worldwide. I was reminded, mostly by Clara's family, that having this organisation name on my résumé was something grand and something people looked up to worldwide, which I hadn't realised in Australia, where not many people had heard of them. But I also figured that, if I could at least get an interview, I might be able to persuade them that I was the right person for the job. I mean, how hard could it be to look after a fleet of vehicles? In the military, I'd been responsible for checking over our fleet, making sure everything was working, and notifying the supervisor of a problem. Even if I had to plan convoys, I figured it couldn't be more complicated than what I'd done in Afghanistan.

A month after I applied, a representative invited me for an interview. I quickly realised how lucky I was to have been interviewed so soon. For example people applying to the health department tend to be a lot more complicated and quite a lengthy process. I heard some of them had to apply four times a year for somewhere between four to eight years before they were considered. I know my role was in a different department, but I felt lucky nonetheless. At that point, I knew they'd seen my résumé and cover letter. If they thought I was qualified enough for an interview, I figured they were okay with my level of experience and thought I'd be good at the job. That took away my main worry, and I went into my first phone interview feeling confident.

That first interview led to a second, and then a third. Eventually, I was invited for an in-person interview at its Geneva headquarters. At the time, I was travelling through Romania with a friend I'd met in Russia. We had to find a truck stop with Wi-Fi so that I could set up the interview with the human resources officer. It was a comical search, followed by a weak attempt to make it look like I was somewhere other than a roadside stop somewhere in Romania when I finally got on the video call, but by then, I was willing to do just about anything to get the job.

When I arrived in Geneva for my in-person interview, the weather was grey and rainy, which made everything feel more somber and serious. Once at the headquarters, I immediately felt intimidated. The building itself looked imposing: a huge relic of traditional château architecture, with flags flying everywhere. Inside, everything was hypermodern. Because of the sensitive nature of the work they do, security is high there, and everyone walks around with badges and electronic keys to buzz themselves from one part of the building to another. It was nerve-wracking.

My first meeting was with a human resources employee. She began by describing the duties of a fleet manager and what the pay would be. Then she began with her questions: *How would I look after a team? What was the most stressful part of my life so far? What does a hard day of work look like for me? How do I feel about cultural differences? How do I feel about taking orders?*

I told her about my time in the military and driving coaches for Contiki: the long hours, the challenges each day. I described what it was like travelling to so many destinations, and how we'd taught Contiki clients our own cultural mantra: *it's not weird; it's just different.*

"How do you feel about sleeping or living in poor situations?" she asked.

"Look," I said. "If you told me I had to go and dig a hole outside and sleep in it, that's what I'd do. I don't care. I did it in the military, and if that's what you're paying me to do, I will. Even if it's raining outside."

She laughed at that, so I figured the interview must be going well.

Afterwards, I met with the person who coordinates logistics for the organisation. As soon as I walked in, he got right to it.

"Let's talk about this convoy job you applied for," he said.

I didn't bother to hide my confusion. "Wait," I replied. "I just spent the last interview talking about the fleet manager job."

"Oh no," he said. "We're not giving you that job. We're going to give you a convoyer job."

I tried to play it cool. "Okay. What's that?"

The logistics coordinator explained that I'd be in South Sudan, leading a team of trucks from one place to another. Most of the drivers, he explained, are South Sudanese, and they tend to get hassled at checkpoints. My job would be to lead them and ensure that we reached our destination safely. That was no small thing. In 2013, a widespread and complicated civil war had broken out across South Sudan. Several ceasefire agreements were attempted and later broken. By 2017, rebel fighting was still underway across the country, and more than 300,000 people had been killed. I figured that most of my job would be using defence tactics and figuring out which roads were safe to travel. *This actually sounds really cool*, I thought. *I'm going to drive through places most people on this planet have never even seen. And there's definitely going to be adventure there.*

I told the coordinator all about my time in the military: how I'd led convoys, further developed my understanding of different cultures, and the languages I could speak.

The logistics coordinator interrupted. "We don't usually hire people from the military," he said. "We don't want you to think you can just go in and start shooting up everything."

I frowned. "If you actually think that's what we do, then you don't really understand the military at all," I responded. "I know that is different."

That seemed to diffuse him. He continued with his explanation of the job. "It is pretty good money," he added.

I laughed. "That's not why I'm here," I told him. "If I wanted money I'd go back to Australia and find work in the mines."

At that point, I knew I had his attention. So I began my own campaign for why I was the right candidate.

"Look, there are three reasons you should hire me," I said. "First, I have passports from Switzerland, France, the United Kingdom, and Australia. With those, you can send me anywhere. Second, I don't have any debts or relationships tying me here or anywhere. Third, I know I can do this work, and I'm not afraid of people in military uniform."

I got the job.

I accepted the offer without much thought and agreed to fly back to Australia, just long enough to pack my bags and then return for my medical evaluations. I knew South Sudan was dangerous, but I didn't let that influence my decision. Looking back, I wish I'd spent more time reading up on what was happening there and how this role would compare to the one I had in the military. At the time, all I could think was that because I'd been in a war-torn country and encountered no harm, nothing would happen to me in South Sudan either. I reminded myself of scary experiences I'd had in other countries, including Africa. Surely nothing I was going to encounter working for this humanitarian organisation would be worse than all of that.

"A lot of places are dangerous," I told myself. "I haven't been harmed yet, plus I have nothing to lose, only experiences to gain."

What I failed to consider at that moment was that, while I had been in Afghanistan, most of my time there hadn't actually been in a warlike setting. Plus, I'd been there as part of a strong and well-armed military coalition. I'd be going into South Sudan as a civilian, with no defense other than the organisation's flag on my vehicle: no weapons and no guarantee that my drivers would defend me, should any problem arise. There were also no guarantees that people wouldn't throw me under the bus at any opportunity, either literally or figuratively. But all those considerations would only occur to me after it was too late.

Instead, I sat down with my journal and reflected on why I was accepting this post: "I have now been given the opportunity to work for a leading humanitarian organisation," I wrote. "I'm afraid I'm doing this because I'm running away from myself. That I'm doing this so that I can feel better about who I am and that it will make me more desirable because of what I will have done in my life."

My other journal entries from this time period also focus a lot more on my motivation than on any consideration for what awaited me in South Sudan. Like this one:

> I'm a week away from undertaking another major experience of a lifetime working for ▇▇▇▇▇▇ in South Sudan. This is pretty unexpected due to the fact that I was recently on my way back from Europe and I was looking at settling down in Australia. I had semi-organised to go and see a GP about my mental health because if you know me, I'm a little bit screwed up in that. I ended up talking via email with people on the coast that were free, but I just couldn't commit to making myself go.

Looking back at these, I can clearly see where my mental state was at the time, and I probably wasn't in a place where I could have made a logical decision about going to South Sudan. However, I also understand why I wanted to go. Another entry from the time spoke about the issues I had with my body, too:

> There was a time I had where I went to a new level of self-disgust. I tried and didn't succeed at first, but I eventually got a little out, but not what I was expecting. I had been unhappy with my weight, and it's mostly because of the lifestyle, but also because when I stress, I eat. When I'm unhappy, I eat, and I've been stressing a lot lately. So, I attempted to make myself throw up after eating. I realised that it's not so much the food, but it's just a taste that I'm craving and want because it feels good. Once I eat it, I don't actually want it.

I'd never done something like making myself vomit in the past, and I'd clearly reached a new level of self-disgust. I had more suicidal thoughts then, too. But, despite how I was feeling about myself, I was not about to let another one of these yearly meltdowns take me away from an experience of a lifetime. I figured I could continue burying my thoughts and keep them to myself. I was scared of telling people how my mind was working, thinking they wouldn't like me for it, or they'd judge me. I knew deep down that I had people who cared, but I had a lot of trouble accepting that fact. I never wanted anyone to have pity on me. I knew people in my life had their own problems, their own suffering, and I didn't want to be another issue for them—another inconvenience.

I figured that all else aside, the organisation could help me see firsthand that there were people so much worse off than I was, and that they had somehow kept on living. I wanted to clear my head and find it in me to love myself and be proud of who I was. I wanted to learn forgiveness and be carefree, eliminating all the worry and negativity in my head. I thought if I couldn't sort through my own issues while others were worse off than me, I wasn't trying hard enough. In a strange way, I was also hoping that, by helping people who were lacking basic human needs like shelter and clean water, I could also begin to accept myself for who I was and stop worrying about all the little things that bothered me. I wanted to channel some of their strength to fight my own demons.

Before I left for South Sudan, I had a nightmare that burned deep into my brain. In the dream, I had started my job and died there in a disaster while trying to help other people. It was as if the visualisations I'd been having, me in the centre of a crisis, becoming the hero, were coming to the foreground once more. It didn't scare me, though. Instead, it only made my urge to go to South Sudan stronger. I knew it wasn't healthy for me to be feeling this way, especially in progressively more morbid ways. I also knew I shouldn't be subconsciously hoping something terrible happened to people in order for me to stand out and feel good. I knew this way of thinking was toxic. But I still didn't believe I'd encounter any actual danger.

"How much harm can actually come to me?" I asked myself. "All I'm doing is driving."

In hindsight, I can clearly see how much I was struggling at that point in my life. However, at the time, I was mostly preoccupied with the ego boost I'd felt by putting myself in a situation I knew most people would avoid at all costs. I thought if I could survive that kind of experience and overcome any mental stress from it, I could finally become the best version of myself. I've always believed that the greatest thing people can do in life is help others, and I knew this job would be a rare opportunity to do just that. I had a lot of things I was still dealing with mentally, but I continued to believe that this job would be my answer; if I could survive it, I could survive anything.

I returned to headquarters to complete my onboarding and prepare for the trip. There, I got my paperwork, my mission brief, my ID, and a blue ID book—a diplomatic book to get you through the airport, customs, security checks with officers, and checks with government officials of South Sudan. Then, they put me on the next plane to Africa.

We landed first in Ethiopia, and then I boarded a smaller plane for South Sudan. As the plane landed, I got my first glimpse of life there: instead of concrete buildings, the airport consisted of a few mud huts and tents. Not a single commercial jet was in sight; instead, it was UN and other humanitarian organisation planes and helicopters. It was like nothing I'd ever seen before, either in movies or in my imagination. When you stepped off the plane, it was just dirt. And heat. And chaos.

Within five minutes of deboarding, I was already drenched in sweat. My sunnies fogged up from the heat and humidity in even less time than that. Stepping off that plane, I could literally feel the steam around me—that, and the realities of work in a third-world country. Going in, I'd assumed that I would have been greeted by someone from the organisation there to help me get acclimated. Instead, with no one to assist me, I followed a line of people through the dirt about three hundred to four hundred metres to the area where luggage was claimed.

The airport itself wasn't a building so much as a tent, and the workers there lacked the technology I'd become accustomed to in my travels. The baggage claim area was total chaos: people were yelling and pushing, and there was no organisation at all. I'd packed light, knowing that I might never see my bag when I landed. But I had also assumed that the baggage claim would work like it did at first-world airports. I had downloaded a screenshot of my baggage claim ticket on my cell phone. However, not only were smartphones rare in South Sudan at the time, but the baggage handlers also expected everyone to be carrying paper receipts. Eventually, I was able to track down the bag and prove it was mine.

Once my luggage was secured, I was approached by my manager, Roby. After helping me clear customs and the harassment at the airport, Roby drove me to the Hub, the headquarters of the organisation in South Sudan. We were headquartered in the country's capital, Juba, right in the centre of the "green zone," which was considered the safest place in the city. During our drive to the Hub, Roby told me that one of the reasons they hired me was because of my experience in Afghanistan, which meant I wouldn't be afraid to see people walking around with guns. They assumed that experience meant I also wouldn't be shocked at the poverty I would observe or the way of living for lots of people in South Sudan. Finally, he told me they assumed I'd know how to manage certain situations if things ever turned sour.

As we travelled to headquarters from the airport, I was already thinking about my role as a convoyer and what that would entail. I could see that most of the roads were dirt and badly maintained. I also noticed other potential road hazards that came from people disregarding the basic rules of the road, as well as the presence of animals and rubbish, some of which was literally on fire in the middle of the road. Every single car I saw was stained, dented, broken, or dirty; some were even driven around on three normal wheels and one very wobbly one. When they weren't walking or driving these cars, the people were driving by on 1960s motorbikes. Driving any kind of vehicle here would definitely be a challenge.

I also tried to familiarise myself with the culture of the place. Most of the people I saw during that first car trip were wearing loose-fitting indigenous clothes and clearly weren't of high social status. The few wealthy people I saw were dressed really nicely and were driving around in expensive cars, like a Land Cruiser 200 series. It seemed clear to me that they considered themselves the elite and would think nothing of speeding up in the streets if people didn't get out of their way. Back in Australia, I called that big dick energy. I'd already learned that those kinds of people are not worth your time. In South Sudan, seeing that kind of behaviour became Lesson #1 for me: get out of the way of any good-looking cars, especially if they're driving at you with their headlights on. Pull over and stop, and let them get by. Clearly, the rules of the road weren't really rules, unless there was a police officer nearby. Regardless of their social status, the people I saw thought nothing of going through a red light, and it would cause intersections to get really backed up, sometimes for hours. I'd have to get used to that if I was going to get anywhere in the country.

Once we arrived at the Hub, I was introduced to the welcome team and given my official phone. Then it was death by a thousand PowerPoint presentations. Afterwards, I finally had the chance to meet the logistics team. They seemed enthusiastic and wanted to tell me how fun and adventurous the mission would be. In many ways, I was still an impressionable twenty-four-year-old, so I believed everything they said and felt myself growing increasingly excited to be there. After our meeting, Roby took me to a nice hotel where I would be staying for a few nights. It was probably three or four stars, which was good for that area. I quickly learned that the only people who get to stay in those kinds of accommodations are either government employees or representatives of one of the humanitarian organisations in the country—definitely no Sudanese. That was my first realisation about the racial and class divides in the country.

Once I arrived at the hotel, I knew I'd need to exchange money. I'd learned that the legit money exchangers took a big cut. The black market, meanwhile, offered a better rate but also came with the risks associated with an illegal enterprise. I opted for the "grey" exchange, which was somewhere in between. Through the hotel, I got about 25,000 South Sudanese pounds for $100 USD. The black market would have been more like $1 to 350 South Sudanese pounds, but I wasn't willing to risk being shot for a better exchange rate. Even just realising that violence was a possibility when exchanging money was evidence that this would be a very different trip than I was used to.

My next few days were mostly spent in meetings. I learned basic protocols, like how to apply for leave or how to use my assigned electronics. I also underwent a security briefing where they gave me information about South Sudan, and I got to see where our big warehouses held all the food, oil, agricultural tools, and other relief supplies that my convoys would be transporting.

After the first weekend, it was time to get started. My job as a convoyer was obviously to lead our convoys, but I was also there for safety; as a representative of the organisation, part of my job was to make sure we were able to pass through all checkpoints. In that role, I was an ambassador for the organisation and was expected to help educate the people manning the checkpoints about the 's mission of getting food and supplies to people who needed them. I was also there to enforce the rules and make sure we weren't taken advantage of while completing our mission to help people. Because South Sudan was such a poor country, often their officials at the checkpoints would try to charge us a fee or make us give them valuables in exchange for permission to pass through. I was instructed never to agree to that kind of bribery.

During my first week in South Sudan, some of the expats invited me to dinner. Juba has a couple of really nice restaurants where they'll do table service and give you a knife and a fork, which most of the time doesn't happen there. While dining, we talked about the organisation's management of aid in the region. They would give the locals food, look after them, give them farming tools, and teach them how to farm. Once the locals had six months of food, the organisation would move on to the next place. Other organisations, though, like the World Food Programme, would give the villages food every six months, returning like clockwork to do it again and again without encouraging them to learn farming skills on their own. Our way was intended to get the people sustainably farming for themselves and to encourage them to be independent. This was explained to me by way of the parable of the fisherman and his son. The story goes that there was a tsunami, and afterwards the father and son went walking on the beach, where they saw tons of fish stranded in the sand, flapping, trying to get back to the water. The son started picking up the fish one by one and then putting them back in the water.

"Son, you can't help them all," said the father. "There are miles of beach up ahead and fish everywhere."

"Yes, but I can help this one," the son said as he put another fish back into the water. "And this one. And this one. And this one."

That story stuck with me because it was a reminder that, as employees, we couldn't dictate who lives and who dies. Our job was to go to the villages, do what we could to help, and if someone survived because of us, that was amazing. Instead of picking and choosing how or who to help, all we could do was offer as much help as we could in that moment. We weren't there to keep track of how many people we could help or how many water wells or hospitals got built on our watch. I accepted that. At the time, my motivation was still mostly to learn and to experience something that most people don't get to experience.

It soon became clear to me that my military experience would only go so far in South Sudan. Without weapons, we had to rely upon the general acceptance that the organisation is neutral, there to do good work. There'd be no backup, no opportunity to defend myself. I also found that, while being in the military was more of a physical challenge, the humanitarian role was more of a mental game in which I had to constantly determine the best way through difficult situations on the road.

The job also required me to be responsible for a lot more than in my previous jobs. In my prior workplaces, I always had a manager or officer looking out for the things that needed to be done. Now, none of that was happening. I had to do everything myself. I also didn't always have all the information I needed to do my job, so I had to rely heavily on both the intranet, Google, and my own logic. A journal entry from my early days there encapsulates how I was feeling about those circumstances:

> It was up to each individual to care for oneself in regard to diplomatic opinions and beliefs, the security, and their own health. In the past, I've had all those things done for me in the military and other businesses. They would organise my day-to-day work for them, like my licenses to be in order and current. Here, I am responsible for much more, I am in charge.

Most of my drivers were considerably older than I was. In many cases, they were at least thirty years old. In some cases, the guys were already in their sixties. The organisation has/had a requirement, which varies depending on the exact location, that a certain percentage of people working for the organisation need to be native to that country. For us, 90 per cent of our workers were South Sudanese and 10 per cent were international. This meant all my drivers were locals or from surrounding countries. They'd had much harder lives than I had, and they had a lot more life experience than I did, too. That said, they all showed a lot of respect for me. I let them know right away that I wasn't there to always give my two cents or to tell them how to do their job. I was there to help and lead, but I was also realistic that they knew much more than I did about the land and the people.

After I returned from my first convoy, I moved from my first housing in the hotel to long-term housing. A former hotel, this new compound contained a courtyard where we could park maybe seven vehicles. Two generators also filled the courtyard, which meant that we always had power and water. We also had a tiny gym there, with some weights and a couple of treadmills that partially worked. Surrounding the property were massive fences topped with barbed wire. All things considered, it was a pretty good setup—at least, aside from the leak in the roof of my room that eventually destroyed at least one of my laptops. Even with that loss, however, the accommodations were still better than I expected. I figured if I had electricity, a bed, and air-conditioning, things were pretty good.

I stayed in that building for most of my time in South Sudan, and it was close to some of the embassies. We would still hear gunshots now and then, but I felt pretty safe there, considering it was all in the green zone. From the windows of our accommodations, I could see out beyond our fence gate, where locals lived in mud huts. There was a market across the street, too, but we were told it was off-limits for shopping since the food there was prone to carrying waterborne diseases; word was that someone had died as a result of eating there shortly before I arrived. If we wanted to buy food outside the compound, we had to go into the main town and shop there.

It took me about six months to figure out there was a bar at the Hub. Called the Jolly Kudu (a type of antelope) Bar, it hosted parties every Friday evening for personnel and members of other relief organisations. I began volunteering there, serving people drinks. I loved it because the atmosphere gave me a sense of belonging. Out in the field, I'd become used to spending time with my drivers. We did our best to communicate, but there was always a little bit of a language and cultural barrier. Also, because I was the head of the convoy, they always treated me like the boss. It's not that they weren't friendly. But none of us could escape the fact that I was a visitor from a first-world country who could go home any time and who had resources they could only imagine. At the Jolly Kudu, most of those social divisions didn't exist. Communicating with the people at the bar, I didn't have to be a leader. Instead, I could just be Alex, and I could just talk—whether I was venting about my job, or discussing things that interested me, or sharing stories from the road. It was a great opportunity for all the organisation's workers to learn from one another and share our experiences as well. Some of us became good friends, and the workers who had been around a little longer started introducing me to recreation opportunities, like playing volleyball or soccer at the Hub facilities. It felt good to have workmates with things in common: we could talk about life back home and the realities of life in a war zone, something that was hard to do with friends in Australia, what with the time zone differences, the difficulties of video calls, and the sheer strangeness of life at a humanitarian base. Those colleagues were a kind of lifeline: we spoke the same language, both literally and figuratively, whether it was talking about road conditions, human casualties in the region, or life away from the people we loved. At the Jolly Kudu, we could just be humans instead of humanitarians.

The truth is that the language barrier in South Sudan had been difficult and draining at times. One of the first weeks I was there, a Spanish convoyer and I got to talking, and we soon came to understand the limits of the language barrier: he didn't get any of my jokes, and I had a hard time comprehending what he was trying to tell me about the job. Most of the drivers spoke basic English, but often it was broken, and the rest of the time, they spoke Arabic. I tried to learn the language, but I soon found that there's a different dialect spoken from village to village, so it was almost impossible to have a proper conversation with everyone.

Without a doubt, my number one priority was keeping my drivers safe. Luckily, many of them were locals who lived in or around Juba, so they understood the surrounding areas and tribes well, which was important for our safety and security. When we got to certain villages, they could easily go in and find out information about what was happening in the towns farther ahead. For example, they'd find out if cattle raiders had gone through and stolen livestock or killed local people. If that was the case, my drivers could also ask about which roads we could take to avoid a similar fate. Many times, the drivers were able to learn important information about an area before even our security unit would know.

We got to see a lot on the road, especially in areas outside of towns and cities. Wherever we drove, there were signs of struggle, like the old broken-down United Nations vehicles with smashed windshields and bullet holes everywhere. But the war hadn't destroyed much of what was unique about the environment and its people. As we travelled, we'd experience dramatic landscape changes from desert to mud to lush rainforest and jungle. We'd also pass through different tribal lands, each with its own culture, from the way people dressed to what they ate. For example, some tribes would mark themselves by cutting into the sweat glands on their faces to produce scars that would remain forever. Other tribes dyed their hair with cattle urine (the ammonia turned it bright orange) or covered their skin in ash. At first, I was startled by some of these customs, but I kept trying to remind myself of that Contiki philosophy: *it's not weird; it's just different.* And besides, this was the most real, boots-on-the-ground humanitarian work I could ever hope for.

Our convoys would last varying amounts of time, from a few days to as long as six weeks, although two-week expeditions were more average. The potholes and constantly flooding roads meant that we had to drive slowly, and we encountered frequent delays. I always looked forward to the convoys that followed the same routes; that way, we'd know ahead of time which roads were dangerous to take and the state of the roads we deemed safe to travel. We also became familiar with where to expect checkpoints along the roads. At these checkpoints, people would try to get money or free things from us. I always refused, and over time I became known as the white man who never complied. I'd refuse every time, and my drivers started telling the guards working the checkpoints not to even try with me; they'd get nothing, not even a coffee. I was not about to contribute to corruption in that country. It might be harsh, but at the end of the day, I'm happy that I never gave money to promote any fraud or whatever else was going on there.

For communication, we used two types of radios: a high-frequency (HF) radio and a very-high-frequency (VHF) radio. The HF radio was handheld, like a walkie-talkie, and would communicate over distances between zero and about fifteen kilometres. The VHF radio was built into the truck, and it was for longer distances, between about five and fifty kilometres. In theory, these radios were great for communication near and far; however, we encountered a lot of interference from the jungles and mountains that prevented the radios from working effectively.

Each convoy comprised somewhere between three and twenty trucks, all carrying relief supplies. The food we would take to each of the locations would be in twenty-five- or fifty-kilo burlap bags, and they would consist of rice, beans, or seeds. We also carried ten-liter containers of oil and water. Oftentimes, our convoys included additional supplies such as blankets, shelter materials, and agricultural tools. When we reached our destination, we'd offload the trucks into the warehouses, or the food would be distributed through personnel and handed over to beneficiaries. Sometimes our drivers or a few teams of drivers based in the villages would go and help out as well. Because we were neutral, we rarely had issues with our drivers communicating with the local tribes, and we almost always had international staff present.

Amongst my regular drivers, I formed several close bonds. One of the tightest was with Adam, who was like the father of our convoys. A small man with greying hair and a rugged face, Adam had the look of someone who'd had a hard life. You could hear it in his tone of voice, especially when he told his life stories, each more humbling than the next. You could also see it in his pot belly, a common feature of middle-aged Sudanese men because of all the beer they drank and sorghum they ate.

Adam was in charge of the money on our first trip, along with making sure the offloading process went well and that people knew what their job was. He had been with the organisation for about twenty years by then. Everyone liked Adam because he was a nice guy, always helpful to everyone. He was also a great cook, and once I took over as the lead convoyer, he became not only the father but also the chef for our team.

While Adam and I primarily maintained a professional relationship (most of our joking around and conversation was work related), Amedo became more of a friend. He and I were about the same age, maybe just five years apart, so we related to each other in that sense, not to mention he spoke pretty good English. Amedo was a small guy in stature, always distinguishable by his short dreadlocks and reading glasses. He had also been in the military before he started driving convoys, first for the United Nations and then for us. I could tell he'd once been strong and fit and that he'd also had a tough life. At one point, he'd been captured by rebels in a jungle and nearly beaten to death. His captors laughed as they dragged him, saying horrific things they were going to do to him. By a miracle from God (his words), an old grandma came from the bush and started yelling at his capturers, distracting them and creating an opportunity for him to run away.

Amedo would often invite me to go out with him and some of the other drivers—guys like Kato, Ayhella, Akena, Salah Dudu, and Henry, all of whom were about our age. When I wasn't bonding with the younger guys, I also found time to befriend some of the older drivers as well. Jamu was one driver I became friendly with. In his late fifties or early sixties, Jamu had fairly light skin compared to the other drivers, along with greying hair and a round face. The rest of him was all angles: a skinny six-foot-one-inch body that towered over many of the drivers. I always appreciated his disposition; he rarely complained about anything and just seemed happy to be there.

If there was something that united all these men, it was the loss they'd experienced in their lives. In South Sudan, it was common for locals to lose members of their family or friends, sometimes as often as every couple of weeks. The circumstances were usually horrific, like when gangs burned down their tents and slaughtered their animals. Sometimes the women were raped then knocked unconscious and robbed. There were many very dark moments for these people. Nevertheless, the drivers maintained a remarkably positive outlook on life. Amedo, for instance, was always looking for opportunities to grow and improve himself. While he and I were working together, his mother passed away. Somehow, he managed to just carry on and keep coming to work, doing his everyday things. At some point in his life, both of Amedo's children had died as well. I never learned the details, but usually in South Sudan, childhood deaths were the result of malnutrition, an accident, malaria, or another waterborne disease. Not only did Amedo manage to weather those tragedies, he also managed to open a clothing store just a short while later. The resilience he has is extraordinary.

By following the lead of Amedo and other drivers, I initially managed to dodge any real danger in South Sudan. Nevertheless, humanitarian workers there experienced a constant threat to our safety. Every month, we'd receive word about beheaded bodies in the street surrounding our accommodations; shootings were common in the area as well. But all that violence somehow felt far away—or at least it did until one of my convoys was met by a group of men with machetes.

On that particular day, we'd gotten stuck in a muddy area on one of the roads. The mud was so sticky that we had to remove our boots while trying to get the trucks out since we'd have a better chance of being able to walk without falling in our bare feet. Nevertheless, we were still stuck four hours later when

Kato came jogging over to me, sliding all over the wet and slippery terrain, like someone trying to run on ice.

"Hey," he said, touching my shoulder. "There's a problem. Guys with machetes. Get back in your truck, and let us take care of it."

Kato was not one to overreact, so I knew the situation must have been tense. I got back into my truck and waited before eventually calling out over our HF radio.

"Does anyone know what's happening up there?" I asked. "Are we okay?"

"They have machetes," one of my drivers responded. "No one's hurt. All okay for now."

Those kinds of short questions and answers were all we could accomplish with the language barrier. Most of the time, that simple English worked for us, but in a situation like the one we'd now found ourselves in, I needed more details and nuance. I hopped out of my truck to get a better look and saw another driver standing nearby. He wasn't one of our guys, though, and appeared to be from another humanitarian company. We struck up a conversation while we waited out the situation.

"Where are you from?" he asked me.

"Originally from Switzerland, but spent a lot of my life in Australia."

"Oh, Sweden!" he said. "It's cold there."

"No, Switzerland," I corrected him. "It's a mistake a lot of people make. The two places are different, though. Think, Swiss cheese, Swiss chocolate, you know." I knew I had said too much from the blank look in his eyes. He had no idea what I was talking about, and I'd overcomplicated it.

"From Australia?" he finally replied.

"Yes, Australia," I said, a little defeated.

"Oh, that explains the good English," he said. "I hate Australia."

"Hate Australia? Why?"

"They put my brother in jail there for no good reason," he said.

"Strange," I responded. "We usually don't arrest people without a proper reason. What happened?"

"He went to a nightclub, and there was a girl there that he liked, and he wanted to take her back to his place with him," the driver explained. "She said no, so he slapped her. Then the police came and arrested him."

"That makes sense," I told him. "In Australia, we can't just hit people like that, especially women."

"For us, it's very different," the driver insisted. "Here, women are worse than cattle. Here, they're worse than goats. They don't matter. If you want a girl, you just take her and go. That is what we are used to."

I wish I could say I was shocked by his words, but I wasn't. I'd been in South Sudan long enough to know how things worked out in the bush and how the locals treated women. Needless to say, it was very different from anything I'd ever witnessed.

"That's not how it works in Australia," I eventually told the other driver.

I then realised that this could quickly turn into an argument; the two of us had very different views on gender, based on where we were from and our culture—not to mention the fact that we were in the process of trying to figure out if we were about to be attacked by machetes. So I tried to defuse the situation instead.

"I can understand why you were upset that your brother was arrested," I conceded. Then I changed the subject back to the problem at hand. "I wonder what's happening up there now. Should we go have a look?"

Before we could, Amedo came running back to my truck.

"Alex," he huffed. "Things are getting bad. Tell the radio room what's happening."

I dodged the other driver and made the call back to headquarters. This became the moment I learned how important it was to communicate clearly when making calls. My message—that we were negotiating with men with machetes, that things were escalating, and to be alert—spread inaccurately like a game of telephone. Before we knew it, there was a rumour spreading to everyone back in Juba that we were under assault from a gang of machete-wielders who'd already cut or killed some of the drivers. A massive security warning was spread through the area, telling people to stay off the roads.

In reality, the guys with the machetes had already agreed to compromise with our convoy; we negotiated, and they let us pass through without harm. I remember being a little shaken up, but all in all, I found the incident exciting.

When I realised that a very different story was circulating back at the Hub, I radioed back to headquarters and tried to clarify.

"We haven't been hurt," I explained. "None of our men are harmed. Please let everyone know that."

After that incident, I started feeling like a local in South Sudan. The drivers and I ate many of our meals together, and I became accustomed to a diet of rice and whatever animal parts were on hand. The rice was rarely washed before it was cooked, so I got used to eating very slowly and picking out the rocks, bones, or twigs that would also be in my bowl. That was serious business; a couple of times, people got evacuated because they had to get dental work after chipping a tooth while eating. As time passed, I also noticed my mental state improving. If before I got to South Sudan, I still hadn't really valued my life, now I started to think about things differently. I realised how important my job was; we were helping so many people by bringing hundreds of tons of food to their community, and they relied on me to get it there. I became even more committed to making sure every single one of my convoys went ahead, no matter what. Even if an entire road was washed out, I was going to push through so we could deliver whatever we needed to. We were truly saving lives with every convoy, and it was starting to make me feel good knowing I could do that work. Just as importantly, for the first time in my life, I finally felt needed. Little did I know that my life was about to change forever.

CHAPTER 6

THE FOLLOWING CHAPTER HAS BEEN DRAMATICALLY changed due to the code of conduct breach that was brought to my attention early in writing this book. I didn't do my due diligence and I simply thought I would be able to talk about what I experienced. But I'm not. In this incident I learned that not only did my prior skills learned in the military save my life but so did those skills I had suppressed from my childhood. Without talking about what happened, I've found it hard to explain to you the extent that this event affected me mentally and also what I learned from it.

Before I set off on this convoy it's important to note that I had been in the country a while now; you could say that I was becoming cocky at this stage and didn't think much could happen. During my time at the Jolly Kudu I had come to understand that a lot of the international staff from almost all organisations were not allowed to drive, not only in the capital city but in their area of operations. The fact that I could and had plenty of stories of the environment for them gave me that sense of importance, and so when I could, I would in my own way show off about it. I wasn't able to take photos but my drivers were, so I often got them to share it with me so that I could show it to other staff members. A couple of times we would also talk about the recent uptake in cattle raiding and killings happening in South Sudan; this led to me reading up on the dangerous work of humanitarian workers, nationally and internationally. At one stage, we found out that South Sudan was considered the most dangerous place to work in, and what department was most at risk? Transport department—in short, my team and I.

In mid-2018, I was scheduled to lead one of my largest convoys: a large truck convoy to a part of South Sudan I had not been to before. This particular area was east of the capital. Not twelve months earlier an ambush happened on the same road and killed a worker who worked for the same humanitarian company as me. According to the UN website, a Bangladeshi UN worker was also killed only a few weeks earlier in 2018, prior to me going there. As soon as I received word about this mission, I voiced concerns about our intended route. As planned, it would take us primarily along a road that connected the towns of Mandri and Marido. As a result of both incidents, the road was red-lighted, meaning the highest level of danger. Needless to say, I had obvious concerns about the safety of my team.

While the convoy succumbed to perilous circumstances, none of us died. Once the initial conflict was over, we encountered a UN military convoy and managed to relay the information back to HQ. Bad, narrow roads meant it would take another four hours of driving before we made it to our next stop. As if we needed any more stress added to the situation, it had rained as well, which meant a high risk that our trucks would get stuck. At a particularly bad crossing, we came across a fuel tanker paralysed in the mud, and some of our trucks ended up getting stuck behind it. It was nearly dark by then, and we were not allowed to drive at night, so time was against us. We were freaking out a bit, thinking, *What else could possibly happen?* While we stood there in the mud waiting to get the trucks unstuck, a couple of the drivers found a beer under one of the trucks. We passed it back and forth between us, half laughing and half crying.

I knew it would take a while before the bogged-down trucks would get moving, so I also used that time to borrow the satellite phone. This time, I tried calling both of my sisters. I didn't want them to hear about the ambush on the news and worry about whether or not I was okay. Neither of them answered. I racked my brain for the next closest person in my life, and I immediately thought of Georgia. Georgia was a friend I knew from Australia whom I'd met around 2016, right after I'd returned from my world travels and before I began working for Contiki. We'd quickly bonded over our love of travelling, and she had become like a little sister to me. Unlike most of the other people in my life, I felt like I could really tell her anything, including the stuff about my family. When I told her I had accepted the job and was heading to South Sudan, she'd warned me to be careful and to reach out if I ever needed to. Now was definitely the time. But she didn't pick up either.

When Georgia didn't answer—she must have been asleep as well—I dialled Tobi.

"Hello?" he said. His voice was nearly drowned out by the pumping sounds of a busy dance club. I could tell by his tone that he'd been drinking. "Who's this?"

"This is Alex," I told him. "It's important. Can you go someplace quiet for a second?"

"Yeah, man. Hold on," he said. I could hear the background noise diminish as he walked outside. "Shit," he said as soon as he was out the door. "What's happened?"

I told him everything. Then I asked him to call my sisters as well as Denise and some other close friends to let them know I was okay.

"I'll contact them as soon as I get back," he promised.

Next, I told him about the reporters embedded with the United Nations team.

"If you see anything online, don't repost it," I said. The last thing I wanted were pictures of me in shorts and socks being shared among people I knew.

Tobi said he would take care of everything. I felt an instant wave of relief and was so grateful he'd answered the phone.

"I have to go," I said. "This call has to be costing a fortune." Truthfully, that was just an excuse. I could feel my emotions getting the best of me, and I knew he was out partying. The last thing he needed was for me to lose my composure. There would be nothing he could do about my situation from where he was, so I figured ending the call there was a good idea.

Once Tobi and I hung up, the reality of what had happened began to sink in. I replayed the ambush in my mind, trying to break down the scene, but it was still too fresh, and I was still too wound up from everything that had transpired.

I found that the adrenaline from the initial conflict was wearing off and I could feel my hands shaking. Luckily I was alone in the vehicle at this stage, waiting for the rest of the convoy to catch up through another tough section of the road. And I simply gave up; I cried and yelled into my hands and punched the sleeping area of the truck to let out my anger and sadness. It lasted maybe five minutes until I saw in the rearview mirror that the rest of the convoy was catching up.

I did later find out from one of the drivers who had been hit that he was near and always watching, guarding me. He overheard the cries but left me to myself. He told me this before I left South Sudan for the last time with a casual talk of "I heard you, Alex. That day of ambush. But you drank from the Nile, and the Nile has turned you into a man like us. You took care of us."

I never learned for sure what drinking from the Nile represented for these guys—if it was superstition or something more—but I believe they thought drinking from the Nile would cure someone from sickness, and would make them come back to South Sudan and fall in love with the country and its people. Personally I don't believe it, but I'm always up for doing something that's different and so I drank from it.

Once we arrived at a safe town there was only one hotel available. Everyone was in the courtyard, drinking and partying while watching a FIFA World Cup semifinals game. Eventually, we found a hotel worker, who told us there were only three rooms available. I was prepared to sleep in my truck, but the drivers insisted that I take one of the rooms. I tried to resist, saying they needed it more, but they were firm. Once inside, I had to admit I was relieved to be in a room with four walls and a door—it somehow felt like a piece of extra security I needed. Our rooms were tucked away from the courtyard towards the back of the hotel, but there was no real soundproofing. Instead, it was a typically spartan Sudanese accommodation: just four concrete walls and an open window with no fly screens, let alone any actual glass. I put my head on the mattress and tried to relax, but within five minutes I was sweating and knew there was no way I'd be able to get any sleep. That's when Amedo knocked on my door.

"Hey," he asked. "Are you okay?"

"Yeah," I said. But I could tell he didn't believe me.

He held out some pills in one hand and used his other hand to point to my heart. "If you are hurting there, these will help."

I took the pills, not knowing what they were and also not really caring at that point.

They didn't help.

Meanwhile, every time a team scored in the FIFA match, the streets and surrounding area would explode in celebration: gunshots, screaming, the sound of smashing glass, and other loud noises. It was awful. Every time the noise would erupt, I'd jolt up, reliving the ambush and wondering what was about to happen. All the adrenaline from that event was still coursing through my body, keeping me on high alert. I tried listening to soothing music on my phone, which I had found lodged between the driver's seat and the central console after the ambush. When that didn't work, I tried blocking the noise with my pillow. That didn't help either. My brain wouldn't stop replaying the day and overanalysing what could and should have happened next. I wondered what I could have done better, and whether I'd made the right calls. I tried to figure out who had greenlit that road for travel and why. I thought about everything that had been taken from us. How could we replace all those items? I questioned my decision to come to South Sudan at all and deliberated whether or not I should just quit and go home. I can't remember how much sleep I got that night, but I know it was very little, if any.

The next morning we were advised of three options: to keep going, to turn back, or to take an alternate route. None seemed a good idea to me. We had been told the area was safe and clearly it was not. We discussed it and ultimately I was told it would be my choice. Since my phone had miraculously fallen between the centre console and the seat, found it and I used up what battery I had left trying to communicate with people back home for advice. But if you remember dial-up speed internet, it was worse than that: ten minutes to send a message, five minutes to get one back, etc. I wanted to leave South Sudan. I was angry. My initial thought was, *Let me call the guys I went to Afghanistan with. I'll get a loan, fly them over, and we will go and kill those guys who just threatened my team and me.*

I took five hours to myself and made a decision. In my heart, I knew I'd already decided: I needed to leave the convoy immediately. I wasn't in the right headspace to lead people, let alone myself. So I contacted Roby to let him know what I'd decided, and he assured me that he would swap me out of the convoy once we got to our next stop.

My decision divided the group. They wanted me to "man up" but that kind of bravado was not normal for me. An ambush to them might have seemed like an everyday occurrence, but not to me. I explained my decision, and reluctantly they were okay. They knew and liked the person taking over for me, so we came to a good understanding. Unfortunately for me, my mental health continued to deteriorate by the minute and I left without telling them about the sadness I was feeling about human nature—how I'd worked so hard to get to a place where I could have a positive outlook on human beings, just to have it destroyed by a band of warriors. If those guys were willing to kill a driver over so little, they clearly had no value for human life. And what about the organisation's representatives? Did they really care about our well-being? I couldn't give any more of myself to them—not when they were giving us so little in return. I was totally depleted. I may have survived the ambush, but it had killed a big part of me in the meantime.

I boarded a plane for Juba with the only items I had left: my iPhone, a book, and a flag—all dumped into a bucket I was using as my luggage. The plane was empty, save for the two pilots. If they wondered who I was or why I got my own flight, they knew better than to ask. I took a seat in the back of the plane and sat in as much silence as I could find. For the entire ride, I stared out the window, experiencing tears and the occasional anger outbursts, trying to piece together if the last few days had even been real. The drama had been so extreme it felt like fiction.

Once the plane landed, I was greeted by the organisation's head of the region.

"We can do whatever you want," she assured me. "I can take you to your accommodation and you can shower, or we can go back to the office to review the details of the ambush."

I knew I still needed to decompress. "Let's go to the accommodation first," I said. "I need to get my thoughts together."

She left me with her driver while she went back to the Hub. The driver, she assured me, would take me to the office as soon as I was ready.

At the Hub, I knew we would have to get everything down while it was fresh on my mind. The transport coordinator had asked me to file a report the day of the ambush. It was only after I reminded him that I'd been robbed of everything—including a laptop on which to type the report—that he agreed it could wait. However, I knew I would forget details the longer we waited.

As the representative and I approached the Hub office, she paused. "How do you want to do this?"

I didn't understand. "What do you mean?"

She asked if I wanted to sneak in the back or use the front door. "People have heard what happened," she told me. "You're pretty much a hero here. Lots of people will likely want to talk to you."

As tears pooled in my eyes, I shook my head no, trying to indicate that they were wrong. I'd waited all my life to be called a hero and to be placed on a pedestal. Turns out, it didn't feel at all like I'd expected. When I was younger, I'd always assumed it would be a moment of celebration—that I'd feel excited and joyful. Instead, it was the complete opposite. I wasn't happy at all about what had happened; I felt defeated and broken.

"Anyone else would have done the same thing," I finally told the representative. But even as I spoke those words, I knew they weren't true. Throughout my short time with the organisation, I'd already seen international staff members treating drivers and other South Sudanese employees very differently than they treated one another. These employees behaved as if they were more important and privileged because they were White, and it seemed clear they didn't respect the native Black South Sudanese. I'd never been okay with that, and even before the ambush, it had made me question the motivations of individual humanitarian workers and entire relief organisations.

The representative seemed to read my mind.

"Not only did you survive, you kept everyone else alive in the process," she added. "We're all very grateful."

My mind began to loop in a circle: *She called me a hero; I'm not. I am. I'm a hero. I'm not. What does that even mean?* I was still so triggered from the ambush itself that it was all I could do to just stand there and have a silent existential argument with myself. All I knew for certain was that the ambush had been the worst day of my life, and there was absolutely nothing worth celebrating about that. *Hero* had been the one word that kept me going in some of my darkest times, and now it had a new connotation—one that I really didn't like. In fact, I would have been fine if I never heard the word again.

I told the representative that I wanted to avoid the other workers and asked to sneak around back to avoid them. I didn't want to hear about what a good job I'd done or how brave I'd been. I wanted the least amount of interaction possible. I just wanted to put the entire incident behind me. I couldn't know then how hard it would be to put any of it behind me, nor how much trauma the incident had created inside me.

CHAPTER 7

AS MY FIRST DAY BACK IN JUBA PASSED, I BEGAN TO LET go of some of the physical tension still coursing through my body. I no longer needed to take care of my drivers or be strong for their sake. That release finally opened up some of the emotions I'd kept buried since the ambush. Mostly, I felt guilty. I couldn't stop thinking about the decision I'd made to leave. I had been given two choices: to stay with my drivers or to abandon them, and I'd chosen the latter. I'd left behind a team, *my* team. I felt like a coward, and what made it worse was that everyone kept telling me I was brave. The whole thing was overwhelming and very, very confusing. My head was spinning. I tried to remind myself that leaving the convoy was the decision I *needed* to make and that it hadn't been a choice I'd arrived at lightly. Deep in my heart, I knew it was the right one, and I needed to let myself accept it.

Before I made it to my debrief with the organisation's head of country, I was brought to speak with their staff health officer.

That meeting was just a formality—a placeholder until we could have a more proper sit-down. For my part, I mostly wanted to see if he had any news about my drivers or a brief summary of my options going forward.

I stewed in the office where I'd been escorted, waiting for the head of Hub to arrive. When he failed to materialise, I got up and went next door to the security office. Without asking permission, I walked right through, asking to speak to the guy who was first-in-command.

"What was said in your meeting with the self-proclaimed general?" I asked him, tears forming in the corners of my eyes. "What did he say to make you so sure we would be safe? Because, clearly, we weren't safe. We weren't safe at all."

The security leader shook his head. "I promise you, the person assured us they wouldn't attack," he told me. "We had no reason to believe this would happen. We had your safety top of mind."

I started rattling off more questions, barely listening to his responses since they weren't providing me much solace. As I did, I felt my phone begin to vibrate—someone was calling.

"Hello," I answered, interrupting the security lead's meaningless explanations. "This is Alex."

"Alex? Hello. My son drive truck. You save him," the voice came across in broken English. "Thank you. You save him."

"Oh," I recoiled. "Of course. You're welcome."

The praise felt like a slap. I still didn't believe I deserved it; all I knew was that I wanted to end that conversation as quickly as I could. Nevertheless, my phone kept ringing for days. Now that I was back in Juba with regular cell phone service, and now that word had spread of what happened to us out on the road, everyone wanted to get hold of me. Family and friends of my drivers all wanted to talk. My phone had never been so busy. Sadly, though, I wasn't hearing much from my friends and family back home. Leading up to this incident, they'd gotten into the habit of waiting for me to contact them. At least that had been the story for pretty much my whole mission. The excuses were always something like, *I didn't know what the time difference would be,* or *I never knew when you'd be available*, but it still hurt. It's easy enough to Google a time zone, and even just sending a short message saying *hey* makes a big difference. Now, though, I was even more shocked. I knew word must have travelled about the ambush. Why wouldn't anyone back home check in to see if I was okay?

After the call with my driver's mother ended, I left the security office. Barely two minutes later, my phone rang again from another Sudanese number. And then another. Knowing they must be friends and family of my drivers, I began ignoring these calls; it was just too overwhelming from a psychological perspective, and I wasn't ready. Any words of appreciation I'd ever gotten in my life were from people forced to be polite. It hadn't felt overly sincere or like they came with actual feelings attached. These thank-yous were real. The people on the other side of the calls were emotional. The love they were showing me felt foreign, and it was too much for me to process. I didn't know how to take it or how to label the feelings I was experiencing. And how could I, given that I'd never learned how to receive love in a normal way?

When I finally met with the head of the country, I began reciting events as I remembered them.

"The first day was smooth," I told them. "We were ambushed the morning of...Adam's truck was in the lead position, and they directed it into the bush. Then, there were a bunch of guys with AK-47s who were..."

I paused, then tried again.

"They were…"

Midsentence, I went blank. I lost it. I couldn't recall the information, and I couldn't stop the tears that started flowing, I couldn't control my hands shaking, my jaw trembling. I cried uncontrollably for about five or ten minutes while the four of them brought me more water and patted my back.

"It's okay, Alex," the deputy head of country said. "You're safe now."

"I'm sorry," I said. I was embarrassed and didn't want to cry. I tried biting my tongue to stop my tears and turn them into pain instead, thinking I could at least control the pain. But it didn't work. I began to feel even more guilty. I knew these leaders were busy and that sitting there with me while I cried was a waste of their time. If you have been in a situation like this, the words "you're safe now" hit differently. I felt relieved to have that confirmed, but it still seemed so simple. Why did it make me feel like breaking down?

I slowly drank the water they'd given me so that I'd have something to do other than weep. I tried to think of anything else at all other than the ambush. That didn't work either. Turns out, I just needed to cry until there were no tears left. I remember a joke being said at one point—I'm not sure if I or someone else said it—but once I cracked a smile, I knew I could finally stop the tears and try to explain what happened.

I launched into a detailed play-by-play of the ambush. At certain points in the retelling, I would stop and actually laugh at the absurdity of certain moments: the attackers asking a White man if he was Dinka, a member of a South Sudanese tribe? *Hah! Comical.* The officials must have thought I'd become unhinged, but I didn't care. Instead, I tried to include as many details as I could remember.

"Once they let us move forward down the road, leaving Adam

behind, we eventually came across a United Nations convoy," I concluded. "Please get in touch with them to let them know not to publish the pictures they took of us. And thank them."

I couldn't control what had happened to us, but if I could control those photos getting out to the public, I'd be sure to do it. Especially as they were of me, without a shirt and no shoes, probably with a blank lost look on my face.

"Yes, of course," the head of Hub said. "Consider it already taken care of. They won't be publishing anything."

"Thank you," I said, before recounting the rest of the details of the ambush. When I was done, the organisation's representatives all thanked me with what seemed like genuine enthusiasm.

"You're a hero," the deputy head of Hub said. "Your bravery saved eighteen lives out there."

I stared blankly at him, giving a slight nod to acknowledge I'd heard him, but I didn't respond. Instead, I merely said, "I'm hungry. I'd like to go get something to eat now."

Later, the Hub offered to send me home for a few weeks to relax and recover, if that's what I wanted and needed. It was, so I agreed. Although the details of the ambush were still clear in my head, nothing else was. I had no idea what I wanted to do next. I'd already committed to leaving my team behind, but what about staying in Juba in general? Did I want to? Did I even want to remain with this humanitarian organisation at all? Or did I want to leave it all behind and get a different job? I couldn't piece together any of it. I knew at the very least I needed a break. I couldn't picture myself starting a new convoy anytime soon, and just being in South Sudan at that moment was tough enough. I'd need more time to think it over. I told the officials I didn't know when I would be ready to return.

"That's fair," said the head of country. "Why don't we get you a one-way ticket back to Australia, and you can let us know when you're good to come back? We'll fly you back whenever you're ready."

"Yes, that works," I agreed.

Immediately, wheels were set in motion. The administration office got me a flight out for the next day.

Meanwhile, and after I'd finally gotten some food, I was sent to the staff health officer again to chat further about my psychological state.

"How are you feeling?" he asked again. "You went through something very traumatic."

"Honestly, I think I still have adrenaline rushing through me right now," I admitted. "I feel excited that I went through that and that we all survived, but I also feel like I can't control my emotions. I've cried more in the past four days than I have in my whole life."

"That makes sense," he said, simply.

"I feel like I can't make decisions anymore," I added. "Before this, I was able to think three, five, or ten years in advance, but now I don't know what's going to happen even later today."

He nodded. "I hear you're going back to Australia tomorrow for a little while. That will be good for you."

"Yeah, I'm sure it will, but what happens after that?" I asked. "Do I come back in a month? Do I risk a similar thing happening again? And, if I don't come back, where do I go?"

"Well, my suggestion is to focus on an aspect of your life that you *can* control immediately."

"Like what?"

"Going back to Australia is a big decision," said Staff Health. "You've already made that one. Start there, by preparing to go home tomorrow. Try not to think too far ahead."

I sat quietly, mulling over what he'd said.

"Do you want us to set you up with a psychologist near you

in Australia since you'll be there for a while?" he asked after a few silent moments.

"Yeah, that would be great," I said, not fully convinced it would be of any help.

The staff health officer and I spoke for a while longer, and I started to feel somewhat better. I was told shortly after that a medical officer in Geneva wanted to speak with me as well. By then, my mind was spinning, and I'd begun to wonder whether I'd done something wrong and was going to be punished or even fired. I started to think they might have somehow recorded the ambush and found fault in my choices. *How badly did I screw up?* I wondered. *Have I harmed the organisation's reputation?* It didn't matter that no one had even suggested as much up until that point; my brain was short-circuiting from the attention, and it kept generating worst-case scenarios, probably to protect me from them.

Turns out, of course, that all the medical officer wanted to do was check in on me.

"If you need anything at all, I'm here to help," she concluded. "Reach out anytime."

By the time I made it back to my room, the organisation's representatives had already sent me a list of psychologists in Brisbane and the Sunshine Coast who specialised in humanitarian aid traumas. I chose one from the list and sent her office an email on the spot. I thought again about what the humanitarian psychologist had told me: *Focus on the things you can control.* This was one of them, getting help, even if I didn't think it would work.

At that point in my life, I had only a rough understanding of what psychologists do. I thought of them as people who ask you what's happened to you and try to get you to understand your feelings about it. I figured they'd tell me to think of a happy place, help me envision myself there, and then our time would be up. The next session, we'd just repeat the process all over again. It seemed almost pointless to me. What progress could be made that way?

I knew going into it with that mindset wasn't going to help, so I tried to be open-minded about what could come of these sessions. However, I also worried that if the psychologist determined I'd had some kind of mental breakdown because of the ambush—something like PTSD—I could also lose my job, along with any governmental or security jobs I might want to pursue later. I'd heard stories of such things—people being denied certain opportunities because of a mental health issue. The message people like me got from that kind of result was that talking about your mental health could also be a punishment. So I knew I'd have to be careful about what I said if I wanted to work in this field again.

The next day, I prepared for my flight out of South Sudan. Since most of my stuff had been taken by the warriors during the ambush, I had far less to pack than what I'd arrived with. I threw the few belongings I still had into a bag and then lay down on my bed, replaying each moment of the ambush again and again. I had a bottle of gin in my fridge, and I sipped at it with the sole aim of getting drunk. Prior to that night, I'd never tried to get drunk while alone, but at the time, all I could hope was that it would help numb the pain or at least help me fall asleep quicker and forget it all—if only for a moment. I also wrote a poem that night. I don't remember any of the exact lines, but it was definitely dark and suicidal. Afterwards, I barely got any sleep, which just proved that the gin did nothing but make me sad and angry.

My trip back to Brisbane was long and included legs from Juba to Ethiopia, then Ethiopia to Johannesburg, Johannesburg to Melbourne, and finally Melbourne to Brisbane. As my first flight touched down in Ethiopia, all I could think was, *Now I'm finally out of South Sudan, and that's another step forward.* But even that thought wasn't enough to comfort me; I still badly wanted to get off of the entire African continent. I could feel the terror in my bones and was certain that anyone could jump out from behind a corner and attack me at any time. I was so triggered, in fact, that as I walked through the airport, I studied every person I passed, trying to ascertain if they were carrying any weapons or might otherwise pose a threat. I could feel the stress rising in my chest, becoming toxic. I knew I needed to get out of Africa before I could even attempt to feel any better.

In Johannesburg, I had to make it to a different terminal for my connecting flight. The airport was confusing, and I was too exhausted to think clearly. Eventually, a baggage handler saw me and asked if I needed help. I was so grateful for the offer that I said yes, even though I probably could have figured it out on my own. It just felt good knowing someone was willing to help. Even the tiniest act of kindness felt like a lot to me. As we walked towards the connecting terminal, I dropped back about ten steps from the handler so he couldn't tell I'd started crying with relief. The tears startled and confused me. I shook my head, trying to stop them. I told myself to knock it off, but nothing worked. It's as if my body had been so pent up for so long that it just needed the release.

On the flight to Melbourne, I fell asleep almost immediately and only woke up when it was time for the dinner service. As I opened my eyes, I saw that my seatmate, a young woman who was probably about twenty-five, was also awaking. I decided to make friendly conversation.

"Our minds are alike," I said to her. "We must both be hungry."

As I said those words, I realised it was the first time in

a while I'd spoken to someone my age, a woman and about something other than the ambush or the reality of living in a war-torn country. I was so out of practice that I literally had no idea what else to say. In the past, I would have asked her what she'd done on her trip, but I knew if she asked me in return, I'd have to answer that I'd just had multiple guns pointed at the back of my head. So, I said nothing else, ate my meal, and went back to sleep.

In Melbourne, I had a long layover, so I met up with my friend Pete, who lived in the city. Pete and I had met in Townsville, and because we'd both been in the military, I figured he might be able to empathise with what had happened—or at least know enough not to make a big deal about it. He picked me up from the airport, and we went to get breakfast at the Coffee Club, a popular chain restaurant in Australia. It was a nice, sunny day, so we sat outside, and I ordered avocado toast. It felt strange to be sitting there like normal, having my usual Coffee Club order, as if nothing had happened. Clearly, though, so much had.

Before the food got to us, Pete and I chatted. While we were catching up, he stopped and pointed at my face. I reached up and discovered that sheets of white skin were literally falling off, almost as if I were peeling from a severe sunburn. I panicked. Was this a consequence of the ambush? Had I become so stressed that my body was literally sloughing off its own skin?

I felt defeated thinking that now, in addition to my mind, I was losing control of my body as well.

Because Pete had served in the military, I assumed he'd understand what had happened to me back on the convoy. As we ate our breakfast, I told him the whole story of the ambush. I tried to explain how helpless my drivers and I had felt, but he interrupted me.

"Why didn't you have guns?" he asked.

"We aren't allowed to," I tried to explain. "We have nothing."

My hands began to shake. But Pete continued, still dumbfounded.

"That doesn't make sense," he said. "They should give you guns. You need a way to protect yourself."

That's when it really occurred to me: no one outside of international aid workers was ever going to understand what had happened and why. Even combat veterans wouldn't be able to empathise with the experience of entering a war zone with no means of protecting yourself. As for the rest of the Australian public, they didn't even really know what the organisation I worked for was, let alone what it was like to arrive in the midst of what was ultimately a civil war in a developing country.

In Australia, there is a very low chance of danger for the majority of residents who live there. The biggest risk someone might encounter is perhaps a vehicle accident or something happening while out partying at night. There just isn't much to be afraid of. To explain the type of fear I now carried with me would be impossible. Somehow, that just made it that much worse—and I felt that much more alone.

During my flight from Melbourne to Brisbane, I thought a lot about how isolated I was and how few people on the planet would ever understand what I'd been through. I didn't begin to relax until I arrived at my friend Riley's place. He'd agreed to let me stay there while I tried to get back on my feet, and it was the perfect place to begin recuperating. Riley lived just a block or so from the ocean, and I spent a lot of my time there walking up and down the beach, just trying to let go of everything. The beach itself was over ten kilometres long and accessed by a small wooden boardwalk. I tried to walk there at sunrise or sunset, when it would be less crowded. Most days, I'd see only a few other people walking, along with a handful of surfers bobbing beyond the breakers. Some days, I wouldn't notice them at all; I was just too caught up in my own thoughts, trying to work out what had happened and who or what I'd become.

The organisation had made it very clear I needed to meet with a psychologist if I wanted to return to work. The psychologist I'd emailed from back in South Sudan specialised in trauma work, so I figured she was as good a choice as any. Her office was tucked between a string of shops in a town I'd gone to school in, so it was easy to find. Before my first session with her, my back spasmed, I could hardly walk; this was probably stress involved and I knew I would need time to get into the right headspace to talk about the ambush. So I walked fifteen minutes to her office hoping the walk would help me relax, trying to get all my thoughts and emotions in order.

When I arrived, I felt palpably nervous; I'd never seen a therapist before, and I knew she would probably want to dig into all kinds of memories I wasn't ready to relive. I kept trying to remind myself that I was safe—I wasn't in South Sudan any longer. But the appointment got off to a bad start the minute I walked into her office. I was greeted by a guy in his late forties or early fifties, working as the psychologist's receptionist.

"Oh, you're Alex," he joked. "We had to Google you to make sure you weren't a Nigerian prince."

Apparently, my story of what had happened in South Sudan had been so fantastical they'd thought I was running a scam. That didn't sit well with me. *Wasn't this office supposed to specialise in working with people like me?* The last thing I needed was someone doubting my story or making a joke about it. My mind returned to the stereotypes I'd always held about this profession, and I felt myself becoming more guarded before I'd even had a chance to meet the psychologist.

Much to my disappointment, the first session went exactly as I'd feared: she asked me about how I felt, she told me to think of a happy place or time, and then we were done. I appreciated her kind demeanour, but our time together wasn't at all helpful. I could tell I was just going through the motions.

Because I'd gone through something traumatic, she also asked me to sit for a series of tests, with the goal of understanding where my mind was really at. Some questions were fairly obvious; she asked how happy I was and whether or not I felt suicidal. Others were about things like sleep patterns or flashbacks of the event. I was immediately sceptical of the questions and their wording. How can you even measure happiness? Surely, it's different for everyone. Plus, it seemed obvious to me that anyone could answer those questions in a way that would fake a clean bill of mental health. I figured if I gave her answers that would clear me with the organisation—the ones that would show I was okay at my core after everything that had happened—I'd be better off. So, when I was asked if I was suicidal, I said no. When she asked if I was feeling negatively after the ambush, I told her it was actually a rewarding experience: I was glad to have had the chance to do my job and make it out the other side. I knew these were all lies, but lying seemed like the only choice I had if I wanted to keep my job. It didn't matter that my answers weren't going to help me get better or that I was just kicking the can of my trauma down the road. I was doing what I figured I had to do.

During our subsequent sessions, I frequently felt as if the psychologist and I were just talking in circles. When she did offer advice, it felt like the kind of obvious generality I could have come up with on my own. For instance, she'd suggest that whenever memories of the ambush arose, I should try to picture a happy place or focus on my breathing. If that kind of thing would have worked, I wouldn't have needed a psychologist—I would have cured my own trauma back in Maridi. I viewed our time together as a complete waste. As much as I knew I needed therapy both for the ambush and for so much of my childhood, I just wasn't taking it seriously. At that time, all I wanted was my clean bill of health so I could put the past behind me.

But, as it turned out, forgetting about the ambush would prove impossible. The organisation needed a detailed written report from me explaining the ambush in my own words, and I'd been instructed to really take my time with it to make sure I had all the details correct. During long walks on the beach, I'd try to work out what I would write and why. Each time I tried to find the right words, I'd have to relive the incident all over again. The rest of the time, I tried to focus on answering some of the more existential questions that were rattling around in my head:

Am I going to stay here in Australia?

Am I going to go back to South Sudan?

Do I have a career in humanitarian work?

Is this going to last forever?

Why are they calling me a hero?

Why does the word "hero" trigger me?

Should I put this all in the back of my mind? Or do I actually try to work through it?

Why this? Why that? Why?

I still didn't have any answers. But I could tell, even if ever so slightly, that I was slowly making progress.

A couple of weeks after arriving on the Sunshine Coast, I attended a fiftieth birthday party for one of my friends' parent. Many of our mutual acquaintances were there, and the party was the first time I'd seen them since returning to Australia. During the party, one of my friends asked about what had happened in South Sudan. I found myself recounting the ambush more with excitement than a sense of fear; it was the first time I'd told the story and felt proud of what I'd done. It was an opportunity to prove that I really did matter, and that felt good. So did the reaction I received.

"That's so crazy," someone said as I finished my account. "You're insane for doing that. And also really brave."

It seemed as if the older party guests—the guys in their fifties and sixties—were particularly intrigued by my story. A few of them told me that, looking back on their younger life, they wished they'd done something important like I had, or given a part of themselves to help others.

After that party, I woke up and wrote my report for the organisation, all in one go and including a detailed explanation of what had happened, step by step. I realised that talking about the incident at the party had helped me remember things I had forgotten in previous conversations. By behaving as if I were writing a speech, I had a much easier time describing the incident than I'd had thinking about the official report. I could just pretend I was talking to the people I'd met at the party; they weren't my friends, yet they'd been so interested in what had happened. That made me feel important, and it gave me the courage to complete the report. After I sent it, I began talking about the ambush more frequently, especially when I had opportunities to share it with older people. I'd been warned by other people who'd experienced humanitarian aid trauma like mine that talking about it a lot would probably trigger some stuff, but for the time being, I liked the ego boost; it gave me something I had always craved, which was to feel like I was worthy of people's time.

It didn't take long before I understood the trigger warning I had been given. As time went on, I began drinking more heavily than I ever had before. Every few days, I'd go and find some expensive liquor that I'd never tried before, and then I'd try a new one, and a new one after that. I was drinking multiple bottles of hard liquor every week. Not even at the height of my party days had I ever consumed so much alcohol, and I knew it wasn't good. I could feel myself sinking into a depression. Worst of all, I was getting angry, too.

One day, I arrived at Woolworths to do my weekly shopping. The supermarket chain had just banned single-use plastic grocery bags, and I'd forgotten my reusable ones. The employee at the register told me I'd have to buy new ones. They were only fifteen cents each, but that didn't matter. I completely lost my cool. When I got home, all I could think about was that I'd totally lost it over a couple of plastic bags. Was that really who I'd become?

I didn't understand it at the time, but what I was experiencing is textbook PTSD. My brain was short-circuiting, and emotions would arise seemingly out of nowhere, almost like an electrical shock. I'd hop from happiness to anger to total confusion in a single moment. It was bloody torture. And what made it worse was I felt like I couldn't talk to anyone about it; not even my so-called trauma expert psychologist seemed to understand, and I wasn't in a place where I could even assess whether my feelings about her were valid or not. I could feel myself beginning to grow paranoid, wondering if I was even making sense or if I was throwing off weird vibes to other people.

I'd only been in Australia for four weeks by then, but I made the decision to return to South Sudan. At least that way, I'd be around people who understood what I'd experienced.

The hardest part about my decision was telling my sisters. When I first joined the humanitarian organisation, they hadn't bothered to do any research about South Sudan or the war there. But after the ambush, they began looking up information about the region. Lea thought I was crazy for returning, and she told me as much.

"You're an idiot," she said. "Why are you going back? Are you just going to act like nothing happened?"

I tried to justify my thinking. Of course I could never forget the experience of having multiple guns pointed at the back of my head. "Staying in Australia feels more damaging than going back," I explained. "People here don't understand what's happening to me. I need to go back and see if I can still do this work or not."

Sonia, my twin sister, seemed to understand.

"Okay," she agreed reluctantly. "At least you've learned some things. You know what can happen, and you're not going to get yourself in danger again."

Most people I told about my return seemed to side with Lea. And the more I heard from them about how stupid I was being, the more I also understood why war veterans don't talk about their experiences. In the end, I decided I'd just keep my mouth shut until I boarded the plane, all the while believing that returning to South Sudan was what I needed to do. And it was.

CHAPTER 8

I RETURNED TO JUBA DURING SOUTH SUDAN'S RAINY season. Most of the roads were too muddy for trucks to navigate, so I knew I wouldn't be heading out on another convoy anytime soon. That gave me some reassurance and helped me manage the fear I might have otherwise experienced. Instead of being on the road, I spent my time completing some courses I needed, like an advanced four-wheel driving course. I also began teaching members of small villages how to drive, which was part of the 's plan to recruit new drivers.

Time away from my regular role leading convoys allowed me to meet people in the organisation who worked in different parts of the organisation. During my first visit, I hadn't realised how many people worked for us, and it was nice to make a new group of friends with similar backgrounds. It wasn't that I didn't enjoy my time with my drivers—I did. However, the difference in our circumstances created a gulf between us that we could never really bridge. Their lives were always on edge, and they had legitimate concerns about surviving that I could never really understand. I, meanwhile, seemed like a total mystery to them, and I think they had many false ideas about what it was like to come from an industrialised country like Australia. However, the new friends I was making in South Sudan had a foot in each camp, so it was easy for us to make conversation or play a pickup game of sports.

As days and weeks went by, I kept telling myself I'd made the right decision in returning. But then I was tasked with driving to the Hub to pick up a first aid kit for an upcoming convoy. The road I had to take was super busy. As it neared a popular local market, I saw people walking everywhere. I slowed way down. As I did, some young guys came towards my vehicle. One of them approached, signalling for me to stop. Then he pointed his hand in the shape of a gun and pretended to shoot me. He laughed and kept walking, probably thinking he'd made a simple joke. But the situation floored me. Suddenly I was back in the ambush again; I began to fear he'd been one of the warriors and had recognised me. My thoughts swirled as I sought an explanation for why he'd made such a threatening gesture. What followed was a spiral of fear and doubt. I could feel myself losing control again. I sped off and drove aggressively through the traffic until I reached the place where I needed to collect the first aid kit.

Once I'd completed my errand, I immediately went and knocked on the staff health officer's door. I explained what had just happened.

"It really triggered me," I said. "Is that normal? What's going on?"

"I'd like you to get in contact with a humanitarian psychologist," he told me. "I'm sure you're fine, but we should make sure."

He began typing an email with a list of therapists available for video chats. As he did, he turned back to ask more questions.

"What happened afterwards? Were you still able to drive?" he asked.

"Yeah," I said. "But before that, I fully went back *there*." I knew he'd know where I meant. "My heart was racing."

He told me it sounded like a mild case of post-traumatic stress disorder. Somewhere in my mind, I'd already arrived at the same conclusion. I just hadn't been ready to fully admit it to myself. It took talking with one of the therapists recommended by the officer before I really understood.

"Back in Australia, you were in a safe zone, and you would have been able to suppress what happened when you were ambushed," she told me. "You were in a place where people know and support you. Even though you told most of them the story, you didn't have time to really process everything. But now that you're back in the stress of South Sudan, you can't avoid it any longer."

She went on to explain that PTSD is like a virus; it can appear to go dormant for a while, only to reappear with as much vengeance as ever. That's what happened when I saw the guy in the market; it didn't matter whether or not he had a real gun. The trauma meant my brain would respond the same way, regardless.

"Okay," I said. "But now I'm wondering what I can do about it."

"We're going to put control back into your hands," the therapist told me. "Every time something comes up that triggers you, I need you to use your thoughts to control it. You need to use the power of your brain to be logical about what is really happening in situations. You know the man you just encountered did not have a real gun. In moments like that, you need to remind yourself of that."

"I think I can do that," I agreed.

The truth was that I didn't really believe I was going to be ambushed again. But in a way, it didn't matter; the fact that I had already been assaulted was eating me alive. What this psychologist was saying was true: I was losing control of my emotions. My brain was doing everything it could to protect itself—and the rest of me—whether or not a threat was real or imaginary.

Thankfully, I'd already arranged some holiday time so that I could go on the Caribbean cruise I had planned. When it came time to depart for the trip, I felt both thankful and nervous at the same time; yes, I wanted to be around friends, but I also didn't want them to see what a difficult time I was going through. I wanted to hide it from everyone, myself included. I also knew there was no way they could possibly understand. Once we were on the boat, I started making excuses to avoid being around my mates. I'd duck out to go to a bar if they were going back to the room. I'd go back to the room if they were heading out to the bar.

Late one night, I was sitting out on the balcony off my stateroom, jotting down some notes from the day and looking through work emails on my phone. It was then that I learned someone from another location had been kidnapped. Straightaway I wondered if there was something I could do. Did I know someone who knew this person? How, in any way, could I help? I knew it was out of my control, but the situation was nevertheless a stark reminder of the dangers inherent in our work. And it also emphasised how clueless most people are about humanitarian work; I knew that no one else on that cruise understood the realities of it. Instead, they were going on with their holiday, oblivious to what was happening in some of the world's most compromised regions. That thought made me feel as alone as ever. I couldn't imagine having fun now that I knew about everything that could happen in the world and having experienced some of it firsthand. I didn't even remember what fun was anymore.

I looked down from my balcony, mesmerised by the dark ocean below. *It would be so easy to jump*, I thought to myself. *I could end it all right now, and no one would even notice until morning.* I wondered what it would be like if I just disappeared from the world like that. Would it matter? Who would miss me?

In the end, I decided I couldn't do it—I just didn't want to ruin anyone else's holiday because of my trauma.

I knew I wasn't doing a good job of hiding it, however, when Tobi approached me the next morning.

"What's going on with you, man? Are you alright?"

I tried to downplay it.

"Oh, yeah, for sure," I told him. "I just haven't had much sleep is all."

"Maybe it's the espresso martinis you had last night," he offered. "Did they keep you up?"

I lied. "Yeah, that could be it."

He suggested we go get a coffee. I wanted to tell him no, but at that point I would say or do anything if he would just stop pestering me. I also wanted him to acknowledge that I would never be able to explain what was going on with me—at least, not in a way he'd ever understand. I wanted to tell him how much I wanted him to enjoy his holiday, even if I never could. *I can't have a good time because I've failed*, I imagined myself saying. *I'm so incredibly fucked up that I honestly thought the best solution was killing myself.*

Instead, I just nodded silently, and we went to grab a coffee.

Back in Juba, I knew I'd have to confront my worsening mental health. Within just a few weeks of my return from the cruise, a convoy was ambushed on a road I'd regularly travelled. We'd always assumed that route was safe, so we were all shocked to learn that the multitruck convoy was stopped at gunpoint. The drivers were robbed of their cash, phones, and other valuables, including things like sunglasses and watches. None of our men were harmed, but it terrified me to learn this happened in a supposedly *safe* place. To make matters worse, I felt guilty for not being there to help and was once again plagued with guilt.

A couple of weeks after that, in late December 2018, I set out on a convoy to Leer, a town located in the north-central part of South Sudan and only accessible during the dry season (the rest of the time, the only way to get there is by boat on the Nile River). It would take our convoy at least a week to arrive in Leer from Juba, and then we'd have to unload the goods and supplies we were carrying before heading back. We were twelve trucks in total, mostly carrying portable houses that would be assembled after we arrived. The roads were really rough, so the pieces we were carrying kept breaking apart, and we had to stop and repair them along the way. We'd been given money in case we needed to buy tools or parts, but a couple of days before we reached our final destination, I noticed we were running out. I arranged to be flown back to Juba to get more cash for us. Looking back now, I think I may have advocated for that flight because I was worried about another ambush and didn't want to be on the road anymore.

The day before I flew back, one of my drivers, Nicolas, approached me.

"I'm tired," he said. "Can you drive for me?"

I didn't think much of it, because getting tired out on the road was common.

"Absolutely. Not a problem," I told him, taking over while he slept.

Before I caught my helicopter ride to Juba the next day to get the money, I checked in with Nicolas to make sure he was feeling okay, and I offered him food and water. He seemed fatigued, which was unusual for him, but he shrugged it off as no big deal.

"Are you sure you're okay?" I asked him again before I left.

"Yes, everything is fine," Nicolas told me. "I'll be fine."

I told the rest of the drivers to be on the lookout for Nicolas in case he needed anything while I was gone, and then I got on the helicopter. While back in Juba, I got a devastating phone call: Nicolas had died in his sleep. They said it was most likely malaria. I couldn't believe what I was hearing. How could I have not thought of that? Why didn't I insist he get tested? Why didn't I do more to stop him from dying?

My mind began to spiral with guilt once again. It didn't matter that I'd never before encountered malaria firsthand. I'd once again left my drivers, and this time my decision had been fatal. I felt like a total failure: a fuck-up and a terrible leader. That realisation ate at me. I figured the only thing I could still do was take care of my surviving drivers. They didn't deserve to be so far away from their families, trying to manage Nicolas's death on their own and without any top cover.

I called the Hub and asked to be sent back to my team.

"It's under control. We're handling it," a representative told me.

That didn't sit well with me, so I called my drivers to find out more information. This time, I was told that Nicolas's body had been taken to a UN camp, which refused to accept it, saying they didn't have the proper documentation.

"So what are you going to do with the body?" I asked.

No one seemed to know.

It was 45°C, and I knew there was no refrigeration or cold

room for human remains anywhere nearby. Nicolas and his family deserved better.

I called someone higher up at the humanitarian Hub and told him what was happening. My job was to take care of my drivers, alive or dead. I needed to have a plan for them, and the fact that there wasn't one was infuriating. It took everything I had not to yell at the supervisor when I called.

"How is this happening?" I demanded. "You can't just leave dead bodies around."

"Alex, we have this under control," the supervisor assured me. "We contacted the drivers and explained what is going to happen. You're in Juba. There's nothing you can do."

That seemed like more bureaucratic speak to me. "What's the number for the UN?"

He wouldn't give it to me. So, instead, I called Amedo.

"I've been told there's nothing I can do," I explained to him. "But they say they're going to give you a call in a few hours and work it out."

I told him I'd call back in a few hours to be sure. When we spoke again, Amedo told me that someone had managed to solve the problem. I was relieved but still eager to get back to my drivers.

"I'm flying back up as soon as I can," I promised.

But that's not what ended up happening. Instead, they flew Nicolas's body and the rest of the drivers back down to Juba for the funeral. It was then that I was reminded just how common death is in a place like South Sudan. People in our circle were dying every month, and sometimes every week. For the people who had been there long enough, these deaths didn't even feel like tragedy; instead, they had become a common fixture, like a sports score or news of a minor traffic accident. In time, my Sudanese drivers taught me not to dwell on it either. They'd learned to focus on the relationships that they'd had with the person while they were still living rather than the loss and sadness once they were gone.

"Nicolas was a fun guy," Amedo reminded me. "He always had a lot of jokes, and we choose to remember him that way."

That, I was learning, was the Sudanese way: you enjoy life in the moment and celebrate it. You accept death, try to learn from it, and then move on. The question that remained, of course, was whether or not I could do the same.

A few weeks later, I was scheduled to lead a convoy to Wau, located about 450 kilometres northwest of Juba. Just a year or so earlier, Wau had been the site of brutal fighting that had destroyed much of the region. The UN had established large refugee camps in response, but tensions remained high. In April 2017, Dinka soldiers launched a wide-scale massacre there, killing at least fifty civilians and leaving hundreds more homeless, widowed, or orphaned.

Since first arriving in South Sudan, I'd made the trek from Juba to Wau multiple times and had always been safe. Along the way, I'd become familiar with some of the smaller communities and tribes we'd pass during the convoy. In one particular village, the kids would often run up to me.

"*Khawaja*," they'd say by way of greeting.

The village was surrounded by large rock formations, which blanketed much of the area in white dust. When the kids saw our convoy coming, they'd often paint themselves in the white dust, saying they were *Khawaja*, too. It always seemed to me like a moment of connection with them until I googled the word and realised that *Khawaja* means "lord" or "master." I would have thought that was funny if it also didn't feel so sad; I wasn't the lord or master of anything, nor did I want to be.

On this particular route, we also passed through Tonj, a city of about seventeen thousand people and a common stopping point for buses and trucks, which always made the area feel congested. On the way into the city, we'd have to cross over a bridge that was about twenty metres long and only five metres wide. With each convoy, all we could do was hope it wouldn't collapse. Although the bridge was made of concrete, it had cracks everywhere, and the metal underpinning was rusted. In the water below the bridge, we'd always see kids swimming and mothers doing laundry or dishes, all on the left side of the water. On the right, we'd see men cleaning their cars and bathing. Immediately entering the actual city, we'd pass a prison composed of shipping containers stacked next to one another. That was where we'd usually stop and sleep for the night. Next to the prison was a large patch of open ground, and prison security would clear it for us when we arrived. We'd then pay them to watch over the trucks while some of us slept there. The other drivers made the short drive to the other side of town, where there were a few motels and other accommodations.

On that particular trip, we got into Tonj on the evening of January 8, the day before South Sudan's Independence Day. People were celebrating, so there were a lot of loud noises and the kind of "happy" shooting you might hear on New Year's or after a big football match. We didn't think much of it, until we were woken up around 11:30 p.m. to shooting that seemed much more violent and was accompanied by panicked screams.

From my vantage point, I could see the flash of bullets ricocheting in all directions across the river. I had no idea what type of danger we were in, but I knew something was not right—and we had no way to protect ourselves other than our flag. I took a head count of my drivers sleeping at the prison and got hold of my drivers staying at a hotel that night. I told the drivers at the hotel to get together in one room and remain there until we knew more. By the time I met with the warden of the prison, he told me everything was under control and that we should go back to sleep. I had no reason not to believe him, so I decided not to take any further action.

But then I heard from my drivers at the hotel that other guests there were telling a very different story. They said they'd heard that the shooting was coming from soldiers trying to scare people out of the city. Due to the civil war, the opposition leader still had followers; the soldiers who supported him had warned local villages that they would attack if Independence Day celebrations were held. With that news, I felt like I needed to contact headquarters, since I was hearing multiple different versions of what was happening.

"It's happy shooting," they assured me. "Nothing to be worried about. No need to overreact—just wait for the green light in the morning and move ahead to finish the convoy."

My internal conflict sparked again. What was really happening? Why was everyone telling us different things? If it *was* happy shooting, why wasn't it accompanied by cheering or celebrating like it had been earlier in the night? I'd seen people take cover. I'd heard screams of fear. This was no celebration.

All I could do was try to settle my mind and trust headquarters. Eventually, the shooting slowly died down, but by the time my eyes shut, it was already morning. My brain was clouded with more thoughts that I was failing as a leader. I thought of the first ambush, and of Nicolas, and of my hesitation to contact headquarters the night before, how I had made a choice and gambled with my drivers' lives. I was hesitating too much as a leader. My morals and values were out of alignment. I was scared I was completely losing control of myself. I was becoming somebody else, and I didn't like who I was becoming.

The next morning, I called headquarters to get the green

light for us to continue our convoy. I also moved all of us into one spot so that we could discuss the night's activity and hear the hotel staff's thoughts about what had happened. Other customers there confirmed that it was not happy shooting but, rather, a violent attack intended to intimidate. We also heard that there had been trouble about two hours north and that a convoy had been attacked, including a fuel truck that had exploded.

When headquarters eventually called to give us the green light, I raised the issue of a possible ambush ahead. They weren't aware of it, so I told them to check again before we moved. I wasn't going to risk it.

Three hours later, headquarters called back. I was correct: there *had* been an ambush. The organisation's security team said they'd confirmed a local military group had gone to the ambush site and were "cleaning up," so we would be safe to pass through. However, when we got to the ambush site, it was still burning, windows were smashed, and blood was visible on the windscreens and tarps on the ground.

"Just another day in South Sudan," I tried telling myself, hoping that would help calm my nerves.

We arrived safely in Wau the next day. By then, I was far from okay. Both the shooting in Tonj and the remnants of that bloody ambush had shaken me more than I initially realised. I was angry, mostly because it didn't seem like headquarters believed me at first, even though I was the one on the ground. But rather than taking issue with the faulty safety systems in place, I doubted myself. Maybe I couldn't communicate anymore. Maybe this was another sign that I was unworthy.

I scheduled a video chat with a psychologist back in Geneva.

"You need to send me home," I insisted. "I'm not in control anymore. This time I risked the lives of everyone by not reporting it first. I hesitated."

She said he would try to help get me home. But the help would take a long time to arrive.

CHAPTER 9

SOMETHING BROKE IN ME AFTER THAT WAU CONVOY. ALL my previous fears of being unworthy returned, and this time they were compounded by the belief that I'd failed at my job. I lost my will to live, and not even the promise of future travel to bucket list places like Antarctica did much to help. As much as I was looking forward to trips like that, I couldn't imagine what or who I'd be once I returned home from them. By May 2019, I told myself it was finally time to confront the looming decision: continue to let my mind deteriorate into nothing and possibly end my life, or get the professional help I needed.

I chose the latter.

The first step was admitting that I needed to get away from South Sudan long term if I really wanted to heal. I knew that I needed to commit to in-person therapy back in Australia—like, *really* commit this time. I wanted to talk not only about the ambush, but also about all the other stuff that happened in my life, beginning with when I was a child in Switzerland and

Australia. I wanted a professional to hear my entire story and help me understand what was happening to me. Believing that was the only course to my recovery, I approached the health staff in Juba to explain.

"I have to be sent back home," I told them. "I can't be here anymore. I'm not in the right headspace. I'm suffering."

My plan wasn't to leave entirely. I wanted to get better and then come back as a vehicle fleet manager, the position I'd initially applied for with the organisation. That role would be perfect for me: I'd be organising and sending people out for the convoys instead of being out on the road. It required an International Humanitarian Logistics course and training, which the organisation would sponsor me to take, and I could do it online from Australia.

I told everyone at work in Juba that I'd be back whenever this ambush PTSD was over, and I'd be ready with my completed training to take on that new role. I originally told them I'd be gone for six months. I didn't know then just how much therapy I'd actually end up needing.

It took another four months before I was evacuated. During that time, the close colleagues I had made at the Jolly Kudu and during my travels kept me relatively sane. One in particular was Rasmus, who also volunteered at the Jolly Kudu and had become a friend. He also worked in logistics, and his English skills were far better than those of my drivers. We understood each other and could laugh together. I am beyond grateful for his help and wisdom. Meanwhile, back home in Australia, Georgia and Tobi also provided great help during this time. I had also started to message a lot of people on my friends list on social media; I thought it would help to chat with normal people who hadn't been through anything like I had, and I figured that I could gauge how I was doing based on my conversations with them. To try and have conversations with people, I copied and pasted the same message to about fifty people with whom I wanted to interact. Those people who just responded with "nm how about you" or "same same" I discarded as a waste of time; they clearly hadn't taken the time to read what I had written, and if they didn't value my time, I wasn't going to value theirs. A few did respond, and to this day I will always be grateful that they did.

After four months, I was more than ready to be home. In June 2019, I landed back in Australia with a newfound commitment to getting professional help. I moved in with two of my friends, Dylan and Emma. They were just beginning life as a couple and resided in a three-bedroom house with a huge decorative garden. The house itself was designed in an old style of architecture, which gave it a homely feeling I very much needed. They also had a cat named Leesie; I was allergic to her but grew to really enjoy having her company, especially when things felt particularly hard. Dylan and I had known each other since grade five, and although we weren't quite enemies back then, he did bully me to the point where one day I lost my patience and had him by the scruff of his shirt pinned against a tree. We were all good after that, and by high school we became good friends. Much later, in 2022, I would serve as a groomsman in Dylan's wedding when he married beautiful, amazing, kindhearted Emma. I often think back to those first days living with them in Australia, as I got to watch both of them grow. I learned a lot from them about what a good relationship looks like. At the time, I knew nothing about good relationships of any kind, not even one with myself.

I hoped my recovery would be quick, but this time I knew how important it would be to put in the actual work. I vowed to be fully honest in a way I hadn't the first time around with therapy. I also started meeting with my psychologist three times a week to learn more about my PTSD. As we progressed through my sessions, the psychologist taught me some helpful tools and exercises I could do to feel better. Some of those tips included practicing a body scan. Basically, you begin by lying on your bed or anywhere in a comfortable position. You then take a deep breath and feel the air throughout your body. Next, you begin by focusing on your toes and then slowly working your way, inch by inch, to the top of your head. Along the way, you record every little pain and every little sensation you notice. If it hurts, acknowledge that pain and then move on to the next. These body scans helped keep my breathing under control and reduce my heart rate. And that was crucially important; as it turned out, I'd been living under a constant state of adrenaline-fueled stress since I was a little boy. I'd spent so long trying to prove that I could be worthy of love and recognition that I'd literally forgotten how to relax.

Writing was another skill that helped me process my trauma. However, early on I mostly focused on all the negative thoughts in my head. In hindsight, I wonder if it's because my therapy sessions were in English, which is my second language. Maybe I couldn't think quickly enough or find the right English words to speak a complete response. With writing, on the other hand, I had time to find the words to respond and process properly. By the time I had committed to truly getting help and working to heal, I had gotten into the awful habit of just writing down negative thoughts I was experiencing or feeling about myself. Ever since the ambush, I had been creating diary entries in Google Docs that were filled with negative self-talk. Every time I felt bad, I would read them and add to them, creating a darkening pit of death. I'd also write poems about these negative thoughts, or I'd write on and on for fifteen or twenty pages about why I hated myself. At this point, I'd become so full of self-loathing and anger that I started to actually pity myself. The document I was creating ended up being forty-five pages of self-recrimination and shame, each page worse than the previous one and more focused on suicidal thoughts, along with ideas and reasons why I should just end it all and kill myself. Although that was clearly bad, it did also give me clarity on some parts of my past that I would eventually have to confront and process.

When I told my psychologist what I'd been doing, she challenged me to do the opposite. She asked me to write down positive things as a way of becoming kinder to myself. It was very, very hard. I couldn't even start writing at first. I must have tried for two days; then on the third or fourth day, I was finally okay with writing down positive facts about myself instead.

I still have that entry. It reads:

For something different, this document will be written in all of the positives that I can think of, without putting any negatives into it. First, what have I achieved? I speak two languages, four nationalities, visited 80 countries, served Australia in the military, and served the world with a humanitarian organisation in South Sudan. In the process, I saved 18 people's lives and served more than 800,000 people with my team. I've inspired people to travel and see what a wonderful world we have. I've reached the age of 27. I've been present when people needed help from someone. I've helped people make decisions and supported people who had none. I've lived in four different countries and made plenty of friends and connections around the world. I explored the seas and oceans, six out of seven continents, and swam in the Arctic, and soon in the Antarctic. I've managed to see firsthand some of the most amazing animals in the world, and I have seen some amazing scenery and climbed unbelievable mountains.

I cannot remember what I wrote in my previous negative document, so I don't know how to go about writing this one. But I'll keep going to explain the amazing things I've seen and talk about the beautiful things that I've seen and done. Some of the most beautiful scenery I've seen are of mountain ranges in Sweden and Switzerland, the underwater world of the Great Barrier Reef, and in the Caribbeans. The walk in a forest and the serenity of being away from anything humanly made is incredible. The noises of nature, the smell of it, and everything else that comes with it is incredible.

One of the best sayings I've been told is when people tell you that they can see all of this on TV, and you say, "Yes, but you can't smell it." You cannot see the faces of the people and feel the energy of the place, the fresh wind on your face, and the goose bumps you get when on the side of a mountain, looking down. I was also lucky enough to go to Africa on a trip and do some gorilla tracking as well as chimpanzee tracking.

These two things are absolutely amazing. The walk may be hard, but knowing you are about to enter the living spaces of some of humans' most closely related cousins is remarkable. They are tough and fast animals. To see them in the wild is so different from seeing them on TV, reading about them, or looking at pictures of them. It's just amazing and I can't recommend this enough to anyone.

I love the fact that I have gone through life without doing any other courses apart from high school. I managed to get through it with all of life happening around me at the same time, and I've grown into someone who has a wealth of adventure and adrenaline experience, which I believe is what life is all about. To be able to experience what the body can do in extreme situations is incredible. Some of my happiest memories and best times have been while travelling around the world, meeting and sharing my stories with people around the world, learning what they have to share, and enjoying each other's company. Getting that ecstatic feeling when you get to share a story, a part of yourself, with others is one of life's most treasured experiences that we can achieve.

We share ourselves with someone else, and I think that is amazing and beautiful. I am also happy that I can look back and really see everything that has shaped me into who I am now, the good and the bad. But I reflect on those bad times and see that I am grateful for them happening, as it led me to now. And that in itself, I think it is very powerful. I need to learn to appreciate that a lot more and to reflect on that and be happy that I've progressed and moved forward. I'm happy that I can write my soul out and analyze what is happening and look at the benefits of that happening at the present time.

It was difficult to write, mostly because I felt like I was bragging. I still wasn't ready for anyone to be proud of me, even myself. Once I'd completed that exercise, the psychologist then had me delete all the negative self-talk I'd written so that I could never access those pages again. The psychologist was very good at her job: she saw through my bullshit and asked me hard questions, all in an attempt to get me to think in a different way.

"What does it feel like when you cry?" she'd ask me.

"My throat gets clamped up and I can't breathe," I'd reply.

She then had me think through what I'd say to my drivers back in South Sudan who'd been with me on that fateful convoy, and how I'd express my emotions to them about that day. Up until then, I'd kept my emotions private. I hadn't grieved in front of the drivers—or anyone else, really—mostly because I was scared of embarrassment. This exercise allowed me to finally do that. It wasn't easy; over time, I'd kept trying to place myself on a pedestal as a defence mechanism to cope with my childhood. I didn't know how to be vulnerable, and I hadn't learned how to identify feelings and emotions or what they signified. Instead, I was always confused. However, I also knew my truth needed to be told, and I had to find a way to tell my psychologist—and me—the hard truths buried deep inside. Over time, I found ways to express the words I wanted to share with my drivers, the words I wanted to tell those warriors (rebels) and the people who were trying to help me. I'd never felt so exposed in all of my life. But it helped.

In many ways, I felt closer to my psychologist than I did with many of my friends and family. I could be real with her. I could tell her exactly what happened—the feelings, the emotions—and I could cry. With friends, I'd feel this sense of pity from them even if that wasn't their intention. It was hard to relate to people whose biggest worry was whether they'd burnt their toast in the morning. With the psychologist, that was never the case. Her job was to get me to think deeper, to look for answers where I didn't initially notice them, and we came to many conclusions because of it.

We quickly realised that many of my deep-seated issues were related to my childhood. We spoke at length about my mother. Turns out, part of the reason I struggled so much with receiving gratitude and praise from the people in South Sudan following the ambush was because I was getting it from the wrong people. Deep down, I was seeking it from one person still, and that was my mother. Therapy helped me to realise that I had lived twenty-seven years wanting love from a person I would never get it from, and that was no way to continue living.

The psychologist even had me write a letter to my mother, pretending I was going to send it. I wrote:

Dear Mariana,

I'm writing this letter to try and help my thought process and to help with my recovery over the past year and a bit. Firstly, this is not easy. I struggled to even get started. I wasn't sure if I would start by calling you my mom, mother, or with your first name. As you know, we haven't had a good relationship for about 10 years now and you haven't had a good relationship with any of your kids for as long as that or more. I don't know for sure if I'm angry at you for what has happened, but I do know that I'm grateful for the bad times, simply because I've managed to have an amazing life and you taught me to become independent very early in life. And, that has given me the chance to experience some incredible things.

Now keep in mind that now those experiences and dangerous activities have a downside to them and this is a result of it. I don't let anyone come close to me, or I to them. I'm not attached to people and I don't like to get close or intimate with anyone because I'm afraid I'll lose them. And well, a line I've been using for a while is this: "How can I care or love anyone if the one person biologically programmed to love me didn't?" And, that is you.

A mother is meant to love their kid and nurture them. And, frankly, I didn't feel that at all, maybe in my younger years, but when I became an adult, I didn't have you. I had to go out and find other people.

Denise has helped a lot in this and her husband too. They showed me what caring parents are. And, that was hard as I always saw

Nick really being an even better kid than me. That put a lot of pressure on me to try and be better and do better; to matter more so that at least I could do something that was above the rest, as everyone had something over me and that is a loving parent.

I thought a few times of how I would feel if I got the news that you had died or passed away. And, really my first thought is *OK, well, that's unfortunate, but she was more of a stranger than anything else by now. Yes, she gave birth to me, but that's about it.*

You raised me for a while until it suited you and went on your way. I don't actually know you. I don't know your childhood. I don't know your parents. I don't know a lot about you or who you are. All that I know is that it's your way or it's wrong. And, that is a very sad thing for a child to know of the parents.

Now at my age, I don't know how to feel about it all. Sometimes I want to play the blaming game and say that you are the reason for all this that has happened to me, the good and the bad. Where I am now is because of you, but I know that it's also not true because I made a decision that I did. I don't know what will happen from here on out. I don't know how we'll deal with all this and how I feel about you. I just want to, in a way, be rid of you. Not for it to be a thing in my mind, to put me down when making hard decisions. I don't want to think about all the bad times when I'm watching movies with happy families, when I'm seeing young kids from school, or when I'm seeing my friends' kids.

Lea has her son. All of these things remind me of the past and it depresses me. I feel happy and sad about the fact that one of the most emotional birthday presents I remember was when Denise told me that if she could, she would adopt me. How is that for a child to even think of? I tend to also judge people on how they are as parents…

…I came back from school after studying for an assignment about Alexander the Great. I had studied for that, read so many books and websites, and I got a good mark from it. I told you the facts about it and you answered with, "If you want to live in a fairy tale world, where that is true, that's fine. But just know that it isn't." You could never be wrong. It always had to be your way. You always thought you were better than other people.

I remember you saying you didn't want to sing in front of your friends because you knew you were better than them, yet I have never heard you sing. I felt unsafe sometimes when travelling with you because you would argue a point with the locals, you would get angry, and they would get angry too. All this happened vaguely in India. The fact that I felt unsafe around you when you were arguing just now makes me think that I don't want to take my kids traveling when I have some.

And, that hurts because traveling is something that I love doing. Everything that has happened to me growing up, I don't want to re-create on my kids. I often think that maybe to be safe, I just want to have none because if they ever said something to me along the lines of, "You're just like your parents," it would destroy me.

In the past, I had thought of committing suicide and a key factor to that was, no matter what was going on or what brought it up, my mother didn't want me or care for me. So in the end, if I do kill myself, the people who do care will get over it, as you didn't care for me. And, that still chokes me up saying it, knowing that you may have brought me into this life, but sometimes you are the reason why I want to end it.

I'm at a stage now where I don't know what is happening in my life. I don't know what's next. I'm worried that I won't have a job that I love doing, that I won't be able to go back out and travel to other places. I'm scared of triggers again. I used to be able to see past the present, visualise the next year, visualize the next activity, and now I can't even visualize me going on a plane to Antarctica, which is only a few months away. And, it's scary.

These are the things too that I remember you saying that have bothered me up till now. You once told me while telling me my future, that I would get married twice, that in between the two, I will have a breakdown and lose a lot of money and then come back and marry the second one.

You told me that I would never have enough money to go business class and to get a Ferrari, all the things that a kid wouldn't want to hear. But the unknowing thing is that the last two have already happened. Although marrying someone has not, but I don't think now that it ever will. I've played around with those words to mean something else. I would feel like I married those people and that's it. And, I even went to Vegas, I think on my 21st, and joked about getting a 24-hour marriage, so that next one would work, according to your prediction.

I can't think of anything to write to you anymore at this stage, but I'm glad I wrote this down. I realize I hold you in my mind and care about you more than I thought, and I need to move on and let you go and live my life how I want without thinking about you. I don't know how I'll do that or even if I can, but I'm sick of it.

Wherever you are, whatever you're doing, whatever state or health you are in, all I can say is that I hope you enjoy the remaining years that you have and not dwell on what's happened in the past or how you treated all of your kids. It's very hard on the soul and heart, and I don't wish that on you when I'm feeling bad, and if you do, then find a way to deal with it.

Alex

I never sent the letter. I'm not sure I'd even know how to contact my mother if I wanted to, but that didn't really matter. Just writing it was a helpful exercise to go through, nonetheless. All other things aside, it helped me to see how truly conflicted I was about my relationship (or lack thereof) with her.

The last time I had seen my mother was shortly after my return from Afghanistan. It was totally accidental; I was planning a trip overseas, so I had to visit my bank to let them know I'd be out of the country for a while and to make sure I could use my money card internationally. While I was at the bank, I saw her out of the corner of my eye. It had been several years since we'd spoken or seen one another. There in the bank, we eventually made eye contact, and the look she gave me felt dark and evil. Ironically, the next day was Mother's Day, and I had just bought a card for Denise next door at the news agency.

Back with the psychologist, I began to get really honest when talking about my childhood. That made me realise why I had so much anxiety about trusting people. As I mentioned before, I had never been given the chance to accept my emotions for what they were, or to have them be nurtured. As an adult, that caused me difficulties in making any sort of emotional-driven decision. Then, I'd become prone to overthinking those same decisions after they were made.

As I was figuring this stuff out, I stayed true to my commitment to take the International Humanitarian Logistics course and training. I made it about three months into the program before I got frustrated. In the course, they use fake scenarios of danger and ask how you would react if you were put in them. I hated these fake scenarios, partly because they triggered me, and mostly because it seemed obvious that whoever created them had never had to deal with an actual emergency situation like I had in the ambush. I quit the course after one question asked me to explain how I would find help in a certain scenario. I told them that to get help, I would walk to the right department and just ask for it. This was not the answer they were looking for, and after a bit of back-and-forth on it, my interest in solving these fake problems was entirely lost. In hindsight, I know now that that course has helped train many logicians and worked well for them. At the time, I was too wrapped up in the experience of my traumatic situation to get any benefit out of it.

Clearly, I was still struggling to put the effects of the ambush behind me. Despite my progress in therapy and the knowledge that I was safe back in Australia, I still became easily triggered.

I'd jump every time I heard a car backfire, thinking it was a gunshot. I couldn't even watch war movies. I no longer had an addiction to thrills and adventure; they didn't bring the same enjoyment anymore. Instead, what had once felt like a fun adrenaline rush had begun to evoke a sense of danger in me. It scared me more than anything else, and that made me sad. My friends had always thought of me as someone who likes to do dangerous things, and now I no longer wanted to even try to enjoy that kind of thing. The risk was encased in a sense of nauseating stress that I couldn't control and definitely didn't find fun. I was too busy trying to save my life to enjoy anything that felt like a potential risk to it.

I also spent a lot of time alone. Most of my friends were working full-time jobs, and my medical leave prevented me from getting a job. Instead, I was being paid to get better. And while I appreciated the regular income, it felt lonely being home by myself all the time. Too much alone time meant that I also had too much time to think and no motivation to do much else. I became a couch potato, and I took to gaming as a way of feeling a sense of achievement and progression. I'd play games that took a long time, like ones from the Assassin's Creed franchise, which would last weeks. Three or four weeks passed with me doing not much else besides playing those games, ordering Uber Eats, and putting on the kilos. I couldn't get past how easy we had it in Australia, where food was always available and could be delivered to your door. Each time I placed another order, I gave myself the same excuse: I had sometimes gone a long time with only a small packet of digestive cookies to eat, and I was determined never to go to sleep hungry again. Each time I reminded myself of that, I'd pick up my phone and order something else to eat.

My old habit of alcohol abuse was also creeping back, and I started taking drugs, too, like MDMA and cocaine. I'd begun to read about the way psychedelics have helped some people in recovery, and I thought the drugs would put my mind in another perspective. I started dreaming again, but the dreams were violent and dark. On a particularly bad day, after having dreamt of being gunned down while my friends were cut up and raped, I bought about a dozen psychedelic pills from a friend. One morning, after Dylan and Emma left for work, I decided I'd take them all. Outside, the sun was shining and it was a gorgeous day. But all I saw was dark and gloom. So I figured, what the hell, and I popped the first pill. It was only ten o'clock in the morning. I took another two pills thirty minutes later.

At that point, I realised how down I was feeling. I contacted a friend to come and see me, telling him I was not in good shape and needed help. He told me he'd be over in half an hour, but he didn't show up. That only further exacerbated my low sense of self-worth and belief that I didn't matter to people and wasn't worthy of their time.

My brain started swirling with the thoughts of how no one would do the same things for me that I'd be willing to do for them, whether that was travelling to see me or even just picking me up at the airport. No one celebrated me on my birthdays or any big events I had. I was always lonely. I thought, *What's one more pill?*

But I took another two instead. I just wanted to feel *nothing*. The friend called a couple of hours later, and I told him not to worry about coming by and that I was fine, although of course I definitely was not. I genuinely don't think I was trying to overdose—I even made myself food in between pills, and I cleaned the entire house, all while crying a lot. By 4:00 p.m. I was feeling really bad. I was embarrassed about my actions and felt like I was a fraud: someone who portrayed myself as one person to people in my life but was somebody completely different. I thought about taking my car and driving into oncoming traffic. I imagined other ways to kill myself, but every scenario involved another person, and I knew they didn't deserve the trauma of being in an accident with a self-degrading, unworthy, useless man-child like me.

Ultimately, I was able to sleep it off. And as bad as that day seems to me in retrospect, it was one that ended up fully kicking me into gear. Within just a few days, I got a sudden urge to stop being a fat, lazy mess, and to finally do something about it. I wanted to prove that I wasn't a sack of shit. I told my psychologist what had happened, and she told me it was common to make progress, only to slip backwards. She explained that many veterans with PTSD find additional motivation through physical training. So I found a gym, and I started training four times a week. The trainer there hardly knew me, but one day he took me aside and asked me about my story, inviting me only to share as much as I felt comfortable with. No one had been so considerate, and he definitely earned my loyalty for that. I checked the bucket list that I'd written in 2007 and saw that I wrote "Run a half marathon." So I decided to finally do it. I didn't race for time; I just decided to run as long as I could. While I was running, anytime I was close to giving up, I'd lean forward so that if I didn't take a step, I'd face-plant into the dirt. After I finished that first half marathon, I decided to do one a month for three months, which felt like a huge accomplishment, too. Over time, I also progressed to going to the gym twice a day, for a morning and then an afternoon class.

While training for whatever physical challenge I'd do next, I'd listen to podcasts from people like Jocko Willink about topics like the Rwanda genocide. It was rough to listen to, but it motivated me. I thought if the people of Rwanda could be as strong as they were, I could be that strong, too. I wanted to turn my emotional negativity around and at least try to use it to get fit, physically and mentally. I did the Andy Frisella 75 HARD Program to get myself training more, reading more, and being healthier in general. I would run and mountain bike or try to find ways to burn a certain number of calories, and I tried getting fitter through the right diets, too. Collectively, it all started working for me.

My therapy was also progressing. The psychologist and I continued to uncover things from my past, as well as current triggers and how to manage them. Managing triggers wasn't easy; I had to first find what began a trigger, which took some trial and error. However, by taking time in the moment to ask myself why I felt stressed, short of breath, or scared, I was able to pinpoint a few triggers that I could manage. I developed techniques, like learning to breathe through a trigger and to remind myself that I was in a safe place. I also began thinking about the ways my ideas of masculinity had led me to put myself in danger in the first place; I had believed I was building a ferocity and the ability to tell anything to *fuck off*. I hadn't considered the real toll those dangers could take on me. Eventually, I learned how to help my mind stop thinking those destructive thoughts, and I grew to believe that I was worth living. By then, it was late 2019, and I was showing significant signs of improvement. My psychologist concluded that I had cleared the PTSD from the ambush. I finished off with that particular therapist, completed the required forms, and sent it all away to the organisation's HQ. I also let them know I was almost ready to come back. But first, I had a few holidays planned: beginning with the Cook Islands, and then the trip I'd been waiting for—Antarctica.

New friends made and first steps on the Antarctic continent.

Photos of me in Antarctica.

Once there, I loved Antarctica even more than I ever thought I would. The continent was absolutely unreal. It was a completely different scale than anything I'd witnessed before. The landscape, the animals, everything about it was incredible. The weather would change from the most pristine day to huge storm clouds in a matter of hours or even minutes. The animals have no need to fear humans, so we would have to be careful about where we were on the beach; oftentimes, juvenile seals would chase us away or penguins would come check on us and nip at us if we stayed still for too long. I took a selfie with five hundred thousand penguins, and I found a pebble that I've told myself will someday be like a diamond ring I can give to someone I love. In short, Antarctica became my *happy place*. Later, in future therapy sessions, when a psychologist would tell me to think about a place that brought the most joy, I'd always choose that icy continent.

I also made a quick trip to Japan to go snowboarding and catch up with Georgia, who had continued to be an excellent friend to me through everything. She and my other friend, Carly, whom I'd met while working for Contiki, were a couple of my biggest support systems. Unlike other friends or people I knew, both Georgia and Carly were major assets on my road to recovery, and I'm forever grateful to them because of it. My friends Nathan and Nickieta were also very supportive. I met Nathan through Tobi at an Australia Day celebration; Nathan introduced me to Nickieta after they got together. We connected pretty quickly as we all had a realistic way of looking at life. During a camping trip in 2021, we sat around having a few drinks with friends of friends while playing a questions game. One thing led to another and someone asked what's the worst way to die. Nathan and I shared a look, and he asked me to let him know if he was going too far. He spoke about five words, and I stopped him, since it was definitely the wrong crowd to be that graphic. But that was the thing about the two of us: we just got each other, and we could say almost anything to one another. Nathan managed to bring a healthy sense of risk back into my life through hiking, training harder, and wave jumping on Jet Skis. When Nathan and Nickieta began dating, they formed the kind of relationship I knew I could learn from. He even took her under his wing and began sharing his love of jujitsu with her. Finding people who think like you and want to build you up is rare, but Nathan does that for me. Nathan, Tobi, and I now have a rivalry where we are always trying to outdo the other, supporting one another but also providing motivation to do more. For me, that is the best type of friendship people can have.

When I got back to Australia and was preparing for my next phase with the humanitarian organisation, the COVID-19 pandemic hit. This was a very tough time for a lot of people.

However, I used it to continue bettering my mental health. It gave me an opportunity to start with a new psychologist to tap further into my childhood. This psychologist and I started using eye movement desensitisation and reprocessing (EMDR) therapy, which helps the brain reprocess traumatic events so that they don't keep coming up or tricking the brain into thinking they're still real. It's been used a lot with people suffering from PTSD, and I can see why; it definitely worked for me. From the safety of my psychologist's office, I could begin to make new connections and finally put the trauma of the ambush to bed rather than constantly reliving it. Using that same technique, I was also able to process buried memories and then more properly deal with them.

Both the EMDR process and this particular therapist worked wonders for me. A big part of this book became possible because of the work I did with her. With that psychologist's help, I could revisit events safely through EMDR and reprocess them; I also came to understand that my youth had been robbed from me. Growing up, I had never learned what it felt like to be loved or how to enjoy an emotional safety net. I couldn't even understand what most emotions were or how to process them healthfully. My PTSD had shattered the few emotional skills I'd managed to gain over time. So I had to relearn what they all meant and where they belonged. Doing that at the age of twenty-eight is not easy. I also learned that talking about memories helps me to remember what really happened. I discovered that my memory of events may be very different than what my sisters remember; our different values and perceptions have shaped how we view the world. It took some time for me to identify my own values, but I didn't stop there. I also sought out other ways to improve my mental health. I looked into hypnotherapy, listened to and read books about trauma, read about psychology and how the mind works, and I did more physical work.

I kept training hard during this time. I didn't do half marathons anymore, but I kept doing Andy Frisella's 75 HARD program over and over. Admittedly, I'd fail at it two-thirds of the time, but I liked the idea of training two, three, or sometimes four times a day. I like the mental toughness it was giving me in return for my hard work. I began training with friends, and we motivated each other. I climbed mountains daily and got some of my craziness back during this time, too. I've always been a big guy, and I sweat a lot, so in my car I'd keep a spare towel and shirts that I'd change into between workouts and other daily activities. Frankly, the cost of water for washing the towels and clothes started to worry me, given how many dirty items I was going through. But it was a small price to pay for the benefits I'd begun feeling.

Part of the continued recovery for me was still writing things down, but now I started saying them out loud, which made things easier. Whenever I'd say a word of self-affirmation, it felt like a weight would be lifted off my shoulders. I was now able to analyze things the right way, understand the things that happened in my life, and accept them for what they were. I kept thinking, *Well, all of this led me to now, so I can't be angry at it. I've done good and bad in my life. Why change the past if a word and action could change where I am now? Just keep on living the best I can with what I've got and aim to do better. That's all I can do.*

By early 2021, the organisation had received all my paperwork and post reports, which included confirmation from two psychologists and my doctor that I was no longer formally diagnosed with PTSD. My hope was that those reports would mean that I could go back to work soon. Unfortunately, and despite how understanding my supervisors were about my PTSD diagnosis and subsequent medical leave, we still live in a world where issues pertaining to mental health are frowned upon in some organisations. Speaking about these issues can harm your career, and I became an example of how that's true. Even though I'd been declared free of PTSD, my former diagnosis made them hesitant to bring me back. That decision broke my heart, because a person should never have to sacrifice their whole career just to look after themself.

Today, mental health is not as taboo as it once was. However, we still have a problem confronting trauma. Too often, it seems like people want to compare their experiences and try to one-up each other. When people discover that I had a traumatic experience, they often want to dump their traumas on me, perhaps thinking that I can identify with them or as a way of competing with me. I've also begun to consider the way that masculinity can make trauma worse; so many boys and men are taught from their fathers or their friends at school that it's not okay to express emotions. Instead, we're told to say that everything is fine, even when it's not. We need to break that cycle. We need to accept that if something isn't right, we can go and talk with a professional; we can also talk with our mates; or best yet, we can talk with someone who has experienced something similar. Transitioning to a place where you believe that is okay is hard.

In hindsight, it's worth noting that all of my therapists were women. During our sessions, I needed to hear about the importance of being kind to myself and to accept that I am worthy, but I also needed to hear some harsh truths; namely, that I was a weak, broken, and sad version of a man. I recently heard a podcast with Cameron Hanes and Chris Williamson. In it, they talked about the importance of recognising gender differences in mental health and that depression often manifests differently for men and women. They also talked about how common it is for men to need to feel capable, powerful, and useful. I agree totally. Personally, I had to tell myself that I was paying a professional to hear me cry and to allow me to be vulnerable. That made it easier to open up. I think many people would benefit from finding people who can truly understand their experiences, whether that's soldiers speaking with other soldiers, or humanitarian aid workers speaking with one another. It's also important to remember that getting better takes real work and effort. If you aren't willing to commit to that, you aren't going to get better. Psychologists are not magicians; you have to be willing to say what is actually bothering you and take down the walls you've put up to protect yourself. Only then will you find your true self.

As my recovery continued, I found that I didn't know what to do with myself career-wise. I was finally off insurance and could work again, so initially I applied for various jobs and tried different avenues like a removalist, or mover, but nothing stuck. I decided to apply for the Australian Federal Police and was brutally honest in my answers to the recruitment questions, particularly the ones concerning mental health and drug use. Drugs in Australia are everywhere; almost all the police officers I know, along with defence personnel, medics, and other government workers, have done drugs before. So I figured there was no point in lying about my own drug use. Besides, I also believe that law enforcement officers who have experience with drugs can better help people using them since they can relate to the experiences and know how to communicate about them. When it came time for my psychological interview, I was asked questions about how I would respond to risk situations and long-term commitments. At the end of the interview, the psychologist acknowledged that my past might make it difficult to get hired, but wished me luck.

I should have known then that my honesty was going to backfire. I wasn't given the job. After I did some digging into why I'd been rejected, I learned that it was because of my PTSD diagnosis and what had happened in the interim. That was proof yet again that, although you may have healed from your trauma, you're still broken—at least as far as the system is concerned.

I ended up taking a job working with exploration drilling in the mining industry. It required me to relocate to the Pilbara region in western Australia—a hot, desertlike landscape with few people. Shortly after I joined the mining industry, I transitioned to working with explosives. I was good at the work and eventually moved up the levels to an experienced blast crew. I'm glad that I took the job; I've never been a nine-to-five kind of guy, and the job comes with enough inherent risk to feed my adrenaline addiction. I also wanted something that would challenge me, and I knew that working twelve-hour days in 50°C heat would definitely do that. Turns out, the heat isn't as terrible as I thought it would be. And I like that my crew jokingly calls me "Danger Man" or plays Kenny Loggins's song "Danger Zone" whenever they see me; it reminds me of who I once was, and who I can become again if I choose.

The mines have also offered me the opportunity to perfect new skills, new procedures, and company values. It's helped me remember what it's like to be part of a team, to work with people from so many different beliefs and backgrounds, and to still somehow come together. The fact that I worked with explosives was no coincidence; the plan was to get enough knowledge to then get a job with an EOD (explosive ordnance disposal) team as a humanitarian. With the war kicking off in Ukraine I thought it was the best option. The job has also helped me understand what it feels like to be someone who doesn't need to prove anything. For so long, I'd lived my life trying to do that. Now, I know that I don't need to save the world in order to have a sense of self-worth. But that hasn't prevented me from wanting to tell my story. Sometimes it's just helpful to know someone has gone through something similar, whether that's as small as burning your toast in the morning or as big as an ambush. There's a lot of comfort in feeling like you're not alone in your feelings and experiences and knowing that other people in your shoes have come out the other side. And I have done all that—and more.

In 2021, I decided to fight for a job with the humanitarian organisation again. I applied for open jobs over and over. I also began giving speeches at universities about humanitarian aid work and what people could expect in that career. Doing so kept my mind even further focused on humanitarian work. I also applied for the ADF again and for the Federal police. The ADF lost my paperwork and still to this day, at the start of 2024, the recruitment has not progressed anywhere, the federal police, they knocked me back due to me being truthful about my past mental diagnosis.

Once the Ukraine and Russian war started in 2022, I went back to my old job and asked again if they needed help. This time, I managed to get their attention, and I got a job as a convoyer. I was told that they planned to fly me out within forty-eight hours, just a few days shy of my thirtieth birthday. However, my departure was delayed when the health team flagged my application, citing my previous bout with PTSD. I wasn't about to back down. I fought their objections and submitted to all the required psychological testing. It was important to me that they knew how seriously I was taking this process, how badly I wanted the job, and how ready I was to take on this new challenge.

Nevertheless, it remained an uphill battle. At every turn, my PTSD diagnosis seemed to work against me, and employees would constantly bring it up.

"Studies show that people who have had PTSD before are more prone to experience effects again," one of the humanitarian organisation representatives said to me.

"Sure, but we also have the skills and techniques to battle it," I responded. "We are aware of the dangers and the triggers. And frankly, the skills that I've learned from the ambush and my past, in general, make me more qualified than anyone off the streets who would be thrown into this kind of work. So, maybe your studies are true, but I want to do this job. I want to help, and I know what I'm getting myself into."

Ukrainian license plate damaged during a convoy.

After some back-and-forth, they eventually heard me. In July 2022, I got the job driving convoys and ended up completing a two-month mission for them, while on a temporary leave from the mines. Initially, I was told that my mission would involve leading convoys from Romania into Ukraine. Although I wasn't scared to enter a war zone, I did think heading to the Ukrainian border would be worse than anything I'd experienced before, including Afghanistan and South Sudan. I imagined missiles flying over my head, along with dead bodies, blood, and rubble everywhere I turned. In actuality, I experienced very little of that. I was primarily based in Hungary, and most of the time, I felt like a truck driver approaching the Ukrainian border. Nevertheless, I knew the work I was doing was important, and I felt proud doing it.

The second month there, I was tasked with an actual convoy, leading trucks filled with insulin. We were destined for a section of Ukraine that was now at war with Russian forces, so the tensions were high. What should have been a two-week journey took over three, due to faulty refrigeration systems, lack of storage space, parking issues, and much more. Regardless of the logistical hiccups, it was exciting to lead a convoy again in its truest form.

My time back with the organisation was fulfilling. Not only did I prove to them that I could still do the work, but I also showed myself. That time taught me other valuable lessons as well. It proved that even though I had PTSD from the ambush and a childhood that wasn't ideal, I could talk about it to a professional and get the help I needed. It was an uphill battle for sure, and I had to chart my own course, one that threatened my job security and livelihood. Ours is still a broken system, particularly where mental health is concerned; I was knocked back by the police, and even by the humanitarian world. But because I refused to stop fighting, things eventually worked out okay. Not everyone has been so lucky.

The fact is that mental health challenges ranging from depression and anxiety to PTSD and alcoholism are far more common than most people acknowledge. That's especially true in high-pressure jobs like the military, law enforcement, and medical personnel. Far too many people keep quiet about their struggles for fear of losing their jobs or being otherwise stigmatised. That has to stop. We will all be much stronger and much better off if people feel free to seek the help they need.

I am living proof that people with PTSD can not only recover but also come out stronger than before. It's true that I experienced low points during and even after my recovery. For much of it, I wasn't able to look a single minute into the future. I couldn't imagine going to dinner with friends, taking a walk on the beach, taking a trip, doing a hobby, or even laughing. I couldn't see beyond the present moment. All I saw was sadness, and I was scared for my life. I saw myself only as an inconvenience to people around me. I felt like I had a negative aura that ruined everyone's good time and sucked them dry of positivity. I'd sit around thinking about those medals I'd received in Afghanistan and how I didn't do anything to deserve them; they felt like a participation trophy or merely evidence of what the media and Australian Defense Chief wanted people to believe about the wars in the Middle East. I also spent a lot of time thinking about my time in South Sudan and the ambush. I still worried that I had failed my drivers. I'd dwell on the fact that one of my men was killed by malaria, and I blamed myself for not checking on him properly. I spent so much time dwelling on the past that I worried I could never get better. I knew recovery is a long-term process, but how do you heal when you can't even conceive of a future?

Ultimately, what saved me was the recognition that, no matter how traumatic it may have been, my past is what has made me the person I am today. I am alive because I was strong enough to weather those difficulties, and I gained a resilience along the way that can help me manage anything. Therapy improved me in so many ways; not only did it give me important insight about mental health, but it taught me how to value my siblings' different perspectives and those of the people around me. I know now that we are all wired differently and have different paths to recovery. I'm more understanding of people now because of therapy, and probably kinder to myself and others as well. I've also learned the value of boundaries, whether that's accepting that I don't have to please everyone or that it's okay to be selfish. Today, I'm much more forward and direct about what I want, and I'm willing to grab it. I've learned to ask for what I want and need instead of waiting for people to guess.

It's safe to say that much of my worldview has changed as well. Now, instead of living in the negative, I choose to live every day as it comes. If I wake up on the wrong side of the bed, I'm grateful not to be sweating in the cab of a damaged truck, trying to sleep while malaria-infected mosquitoes bite me and my stomach rumbles from only having eaten three digestive cookies the day before. I think about the future all the time now—a stark difference from how I viewed things for far too long. I still stress about things, and I'm anxious about what might come, but I can also envision all the amazing things I'll do tomorrow or fifty years from now. Meanwhile, I don't beat myself up for not having all the answers or knowing exactly what I want to do with my life. I'm thankful for at least having forethought again. And now that I've ticked everything off my old bucket list, I've even created a new one with even more ludicrous challenges to keep me busy for the next decade.

If you or someone you know has PTSD, don't give up hope. I am living proof that there is a path to healing and recovery. The future doesn't have to be bleak, and you can still live the life you've always dreamed about. The first step forward is acknowledging that it's okay to get help. The second is making a commitment to getting the help you need. It doesn't matter where you are in your life or how old you are. The future is still waiting for you. In fact, one of my favourite quotes is by the Australian film director Baz Luhrmann. He once said, "The most interesting people I know didn't know at twenty-two what they wanted to do with their lives, and some of the most interesting forty-year-olds I know still don't." That's okay, adds Luhrmann. What matters is that we take time to enjoy the bodies we've been given and the lives that lay before us.

Speaking personally, I'm no longer worried about where I'm going or what will happen when I'm gone. Instead, I'm focused on experiencing the world and what it has to offer. I'm realistic that my mental health will be an ongoing journey, just like everyone else's. For instance, the past year has had some setbacks, but this time I knew how to manage them. I have my techniques like the body scan and a great support system, including my friends Tobi, Georgia, Nathan, and Carly, as well as scores of other people I can call upon. The real difference now is that I'm confident I have the tools I need to get better.

I'd like to say I have it all figured out now, but I'd be lying. Even today, having gone through a lot of therapy, it's still difficult for me to accept love. Having to verbalise it still makes my throat clench up, although my body is finally trying to accept it. There's still a conflict within me: part of me truly wants to be accepted, and the other part feels like I'd gone so many years without love that I no longer need it. I have to process this conflict in small chunks whenever it appears. The important thing is that I don't beat myself up over it anymore. I've accepted that loving yourself is the same as loving someone else (or at least that's how I see it). I wouldn't love someone else who is lazy, unproductive, and disloyal. So why would I believe the lie that we should love ourselves no matter what? No, I will work hard, discipline myself, be loyal to friends, and prioritise myself over others.

When I first decided to put my words on paper and in a memoir, I hoped it would help people see the power of asking for help and inspire them to commit to receiving it. I also hoped people would see that recovery from any kind of mental health issue is not a one-size-fits-all situation. Instead, treatment is as unique as we all are. If there's one thing we can all share in common, it's that getting better will undoubtedly take more time than you want or think it will take. For me, it required a combination of therapists I'd found strength in, along with friends who were genuinely there for me, once I finally decided to let them in. And it was absolutely worth the wait.

Writing this memoir has become a way of inspiring, helping, and motivating people, including myself. I want it to remind all of us to keep moving forward, to learn from our experiences and failures, and to keep striving for everything we want. We all need to stay open to new experiences, even when they challenge us.

Mental health is ever changing. The first version of this book came across to me as a victim mindset; there were no masculine traits that I could see. We men don't talk about these things. Our ancestors were definitely stronger. We lived in harder times then and unfortunately we live in easier times now. I need to train and harden the fuck up, as we say. What's done is done however, and my hope is that this book and its messages last far longer than I will and that I will finally reach a place where I can put the story of my ambush in the past.

I've finally begun to understand what life is like without having to constantly put myself on a pedestal. I'm starting to envision what my life might look like if I settle down. I've started to remove the tendency to be so harsh with myself, and I've learned how to channel those feelings into more helpful motivation. Being a little harsh on myself here and there makes me take action, and in many ways, it has saved my life.

I hope that whatever you're going through, you find something to be proud of and that you share it with me and others. I hope that you do what you're passionate about, because that is where each of us thrives. Do something great, and you won't regret it. Find your purpose, knowing that it could take a lifetime. Know that you're worthy.

I can't wait to see what comes next for me, too. Now that I'm constantly thinking about the future again, I'm ready for new goals, new adventures, and new memories because in the end, what are we but just memories? If I had to bet, I'm guessing they'll be whatever gives me a major rush. Some old habits never die.

www.ingramcontent.com/pod-product-compliance
Lightning Source LLC
Chambersburg PA
CBHW060523080526
44586CB00012B/591